Coming Out of the Tunnel

The Journey of My Life

By Florence Diana Hunt, DA

DEDICATION

There are so many people to whom I owe thanks. First and foremost, thank you to my late grandmother. Granny always told me that someday I would write a book about my life. I never believed her. I should have. She was always right.

To my late mother: I know you learned your parenting skills late in life. I appreciate the time we had when you were, indeed, my mother. Thank you. I'm glad that, along the way, you found some peace and reconciliation within yourself.

To someone special who believed in me at some of the worst moments of my life. Thank you. Those words are so insignificant, but they are heartfelt. Though you went through trials of your own, you always made time for me; I will always be there for you. Dario, you have a special place in my heart. You are my 'grand passion.' If I could 'write' the future, you would have been there and a part of it. I can't imagine life without you. I miss you so much.

To all my professors, thank you; I honor all of you. I could not have done this without the encouragement and support that was shown to me while I was a student.

Special thanks to Jeff Berman, whose own courage inspired me in ways unimaginable. You made me believe I could do this. I owe you.

To my students, thank you. I get to see the world through the eyes of youth. How lucky can I be to be able to do that anew every semester?

To everyone who has touched my life, good or bad, I am stronger because of my experiences with each of you.

To Tommy Farese, formerly of Trans-Siberian Orchestra... thank you for giving Christmas back to me in a simple act of kindness.

To my family: I am proud to be related to all of you.

A special thank you to my children: I love you lots!

To Dr. Serlin who believed a crazy story and probably saved my life.

To those reading about this journey I have lived, ride through the tunnel with me. Think, as you look out the windows of my life, about your own journey. Apply lessons learned by me to your own experiences. You may find many similarities here. We are all living our lives in the tunnel. Look, as you see the points where all light, hope, is cut off. See, the dim shadows of light trying to fight its way into the blackness of life's tunnel at its darkest moments. Experience the moment where the light envelops the darkness and swallows it whole...

The light shines through!

PREFACE

This story, my story, was not one that I imagined would ever be put into words on paper. Rather, I believed it was enough to have lived it; at times, even living it was more than I could bear. I did not foresee this written version. Had I done so, I would have remembered more ... or less. Therefore, I am calling this 'fiction' based on fact. I will, for effect and constraints of time, and paper, condense some incidents. For privacy and legal necessity, I will change some names. But, this is my story, my life, here on these pages for all to see: family, friends, enemies, acquaintances, peers, and my unknown readers.

I hope my life will inspire some who read or hear my story. I hope I will be clarifying my actions, good or bad, for those who know me. I hope some will see themselves in the words and know that they are not alone. I hope some realize the complexities of thought, word, and deed that make up a human being. I hope, beyond all else, that my life will make a difference in the lives of my readers. I hope that they may take some part of it away with them and change and improve their own lives.

Florence Diana Hunt

Coming Out of the Tunnel

Table of Contents:

The Time Before the Crash

A child is born into chaos. What chance in life did she have? If the tone of one's life is set from the beginning, what can this child become? What will this child learn from life?

A little girl was on her grandfather's knee; they read, or as he said proudly, they "perused the periodicals." They, both of them together, worked as a team drawing conclusions from the newspapers. Mostly it was his conclusions from years of scooping in knowledge and depositing it in, what she believed then, was the biggest brain in the world. He would say, "We are doomed to repeat the mistake of the past unless we learn from the past, because humans tend never to learn. You, my love, must learn."[1] She did not know he was referring to the history of one's own life. She always listened to him. To her he was always right no matter what. Her education had begun during these quiet moments. She learned trust.

1 This was my grandfather's version of a quote by Santayana: "Those who cannot remember the past are condemned to repeat it." The Life of Reason.

Though she had met him for the first time three years ago, she saw him for the first time today. He was tall, smiling, friendly, and handsome. Twelve years to her seven. Most importantly, he was to be her future husband. That summer, she fell as in love with him as only a seven year old could. He protected her. He took her to magical places: castles, woods, medieval churches, fields of heather that looked like fairies inhabiting the dainty amethyst buds. It was here; in her childlike version of courtly love she became enamored with princesses and princes. She learned love.

Oh so much wiser now ... she thought. Life between two continents had broadened her mind ... she believed. She had loving grandparents on one side of "the pond" and a loving aunt and uncle on the other side. She had learned love and trust. She thought she knew the real meaning of life. It was this thought, and the new man in her life, who led her to make her first difficult choice in life. After all, betrothals were so old fashioned. He would understand that they shared fairytales and castles and she wanted to live in the real world now. She learned independence.

Her daughter was lying on her side facing the door. What a beautiful little angel she was lying there in sleep. Her arm stuck out from under the covers and rested next to her face, tangled in the sandy blonde curls on the pillow. She was a beauty at six years old. It was the last time she would see her daughter sleeping in her own bed. The doctors said it was Reyes Syndrome. The death was quick. A few days of tubes and wires and the smell of the ICU and a precious little life was over. She learned grief.

The marriage had ended as quickly as the death of her daughter. It was just her and her son now. Quietly, in the hours before dawn as the world was preparing to awaken, darkness came again for her. The police were patient as they explained to her eight year old son how his father died. They did not tell him he was drunk - until he asked. They told him how fast his father was going. Death was instantaneous. Tree ... Motorcycle ... Crash. She learned loneliness.

It was his smile. The way his mouth moved when he did it. The smile shone from his eyes and lit her world again. She wasn't looking for it. She was grieving again. Death had come into her life again. Though not very close to her mother until later years, they had been recently. Breast cancer took the budding closeness, denied in childhood, away forever. Love helped her recover. A whirlwind romance followed by a special wedding to begin life again. She learned contentment.

Coming Out of the Tunnel

PHOTOS:

Seeing the Light

The young boy looked out of the cold, curved window of the plane. He saw the flowing waters of the Thames encircling the green carpet of the countryside panorama below him. The majestic stone castle known as the Queen's favorite residence, Windsor, came into the view of the wide inquisitive eyes. The rambling and beautiful structures of the castle made him stare in wide eyed wonder. Suddenly, she came into view. Flying low in the flight path over Great Windsor Park sometimes let passengers catch private glimpses. The young boy saw one of these now. Sitting in the grass was a woman. From this height, it was unclear who she was or how old. She looked regal to the young boy. Her skirt spread around her in splashes of purple floating on a sea of green. She was surrounded by a beautiful garden deep within the walls of the castle. The young boy, mesmerized, reached behind him and tugged on his mother's sleeve. "Mummy! I see a princess!" he shouted. His mother leaned in close to the window and looked out on the pastoral scene drifting slowly out of view. "Yes dear, I think you might have seen just that." She whispered softly to her son. "Do they have Princesses in America mummy?" he questioned innocently. They might dear, they might."

The Time Before the Crash

CHAPTER ONE - June 1952

The night was hot and humid. Breathing was reminiscent of walking from the cool, skin-tingling comfort of central air into the oppressive heat of a Florida summer. Lil, eight and a half months pregnant, was having a very hard time finding a position for bodily comfort, let alone comfortable breathing. Beads of perspiration ran down the small of her back and pooled in the small valley between her breasts and her swollen belly. Sitting on the edge of her bunk with her hands on her lower back, she moaned. She knew no one would hear her.

Bedford Hills Correctional Institution, a women's prison in New York, was a cacophony of noise at night. As she sat, eyes closed, head raised to catch a rare stray breeze, she listened. The sounds were almost tangible, like the air. The loudest was the sound of the new inmate. She was young and scared and screamed for her mother, in her sleep, every night - the screams of fear. The other screams were those of anger. They were the screams and staccato bursts of fists against bars, one of the many fights that happened nightly, echoed down the hall, bouncing from cell to cell as pillows covered heads that tried to dream of the outside world... outside here.

Soft sounds came to Lil too. These were the soft, moaning, passionate sounds of lovemaking. Lil shifted her position and the first contraction hit. She arched her back and screamed. The noises around her stopped. The corridor of the prison was deathly silent. Suddenly, there were cheers. "Way to go Lil!" "Hang in there, honey!" "You'll get good drugs now!" "You'll get outta here for a while, sweetie!" "You don't want no nurse, ya hear? Tell 'em ya wants a doctor now." Voice after voice came to her in the tiny cell.

The commotion caused the guard, usually reading her favorite gossip rag at this time, to come padding down the long mud-green hall. Lights, caged in wire that seemed not only to protect the bulbs, but imprison the glow itself, loomed over her every step. Her shadow stretched before her, announcing her arrival to each cell along the dingy corridor. A waddling shadow then a waddling person rambled past each cell slowly.

Peeking into Lil's cell, almost hesitantly and with a fear of what she would see, the guard said, "Lil, is it your time now?" "Yes," hissed Lil through clenched teeth. Another contraction had hit, and the effort to breathe in the heat was replaced with the effort to breathe through the pain. "I'll call for the ambulance and come back with the matron," the guard said quietly." She shuffled back to the guard room relieved by the fact there was time enough to get this one out of here before she delivered. No mess on her watch!

Now you could hear the chatter of women. They talked about the commonality they all had at this moment. Birth. The pains they had during labor. The doctors' mistakes, the nurses who held their hands, the husbands who never came, the husbands who did, many tales of many times in many voices.

The ambulance took Lil into the night. Like a white womb, it slowly glided through the dark night and delivered Lil to the hospital. She was to give birth here at Grasslands Hospital.1 Grasslands was used for all prisoner's giving birth because the prison lacked the facilities needed if anything went wrong. Lil knew that in a week she would be back in prison to serve the rest of her sentence. The baby would remain at the hospital. In a few months, Lil would leave here. She had plans. They did not, however, include a baby. Now, though, was not the time to deal with that issue. Now, all Lil wanted was to do was get this damn baby out of her.

On a sunny and bright morning, a tiny baby girl came into this world. It was a hot June day in Valhalla. Valhalla was not the home of the gods, but a town in New York. She was not a goddess, just a Rosebud. The nursing staff had given her that nickname while waiting for her given name to be decided. Pink, tiny, and forever furling and unfurling her little body and tiny clenched hands, she was like a rose in eternal bloom. Her first breath had been drawn in the delivery room at Grasslands Hospital, now called Westchester County Medical Center, in upstate New York. She had arrived.

A few days later, Lil had gone back to Bedford Hills.2 Grudgingly, almost unwillingly, before she left the hospital she called her mother, Lillian. The hospital was insistent. Plans would have to be made for this little one. Someone had to do it. The baby could not be released without a safe and prepared place at the ready. Had she been able, Lil would have served her remaining time and left without a word to family – without a stop at that hospital. "Someone would have figured out what to do with that baby," she thought.

Rosebud had more than her 'three strikes' against her from the start. She was illegitimate, a bastard. Her mother, in prison for grand theft, was also recently divorced. Her ex-husband was not Rosebud's father. A fact he had written into the divorce papers. He did not want to be forced to care for this baby financially. Lil had lied to him multiple times. As all lies do, Lil's lies finally caught up to her. Her ex was now free and she was in prison. Lil knew who Rosebud's father was, but would not name him for reasons of her own. There were guesses and assumptions, but Lil remained mute. She would take the secret to her grave.

The chaos and confusion of coming into the world, eased only by a stay in the hospital until her mother finished the final few months of a mandatory sentence, proved to be a continuing theme in Rosebud's life. Chaos and confusion followed Rosebud for a very long time. Her young life would be driven by it.

The decision makers at this extraordinary beginning of Rosebud's life were her grandmother, Lillian, and great-grandmother, Emily. After the call from Lil, plans had been made, and baby furniture had been bought. Necessities for mother and child were lovingly chosen and cooed over. The two women had decided that mother and daughter would live under Emily's roof. "After all," Emily said to her daughter Lillian, "this is the most prudent thing to do. I will be in England at least seven months of the year. Lil will feel she has her space with the baby. We know how she is when she feels constrained, don't we dear?"

Lillian shook her head in agreement. Yes, everyone knew how Lil reacted when she felt forced into a situation she did not like. She removed herself...quickly and silently, if you were lucky. Sometimes she acted out in ways that the very proper English family she was born into had no basis for understanding. In polite society, Lil would be called temperamental. Many just called her a cold, heartless, bitch. Both views were correct. The women had set up the nursery and happily awaited the new baby's arrival.

Lil's sentence was coming to its end. Plans to retrieve both mother and daughter had been made and then hastily cancelled. Lil wanted no one to come. She had made her own plans to come home. These plans did not include forced conversation and questions she did not want to answer. No, Lil had already made plans ...other plans. Her plans.

If any of the family had stopped to think about the way the new mother chose to live her life to that moment, they would have foreseen what happened next.

Lil was hard to control from the start of her life. The oldest of four children, two girls and two boys, she was notoriously independent. This had resulted in a rebelliousness that encouraged truancy in her teen years. At the time, the parents of children who were chronically truant could be jailed and fined. Lil's parents, having no recourse after appearing before a judge, had decided a juvenile detention center was the only way to handle their rebellious daughter. This step, however, had only introduced their thirteen year old daughter to new forms of rebellion and a new, but equally rebellious, group of friends. By the time Lil came home, at sixteen, life was never the same for her parents.

The expectation of actually having Lil return to the family and conform to the role of a parent was too much to expect. To Lil's credit, she did not abandon her baby in the hospital, as she had originally intended. She did not leave her baby in a trash bin. She did not sell her baby for drugs, although she used them. Nor did she barter her for money. She brought Rosebud to her grandmother's home, took everything of value she could, and left the sleeping and unaware baby in her new crib. Rosebud was not of value. Lil was gone in minutes without a backward glance to the sleeping infant.

Lillian took on the task of raising yet another child. Rosebud's new things were moved to her grandmother's home, and she was in another new place once again. The family she had been born into was a large, loving, and close one. The family lived on two sides of the Atlantic: Ridgewood, Queens, New York and Lee-on-the-Solent, Hampshire, England. Her great-grandmother, a British citizen, had four children of her own. She had chosen to split her family in a unique and advantageous way. She left a son and a daughter in England and brought a son and a daughter to America. All her grown children found mates and set up households. Emily accomplished what she had intended. She wanted to be able to travel between both places and have a place to stay in both once she arrived.

This choice, made long before Rosebud's new little life came along, was to influence her life profoundly in the future. But, for now, it made one thing possible – travel. Rosebud would grow up with a love of both places. This love became a haven for her, but she never realized how it would eventually help her build a new life. For now, she was in a place of comfort and love. A fuss was made of her in the usual 'new baby' way. She did not realize she had been abandoned by her mother. She would, eventually, and at a very young age. For now she knew love and safety. She knew comfort and warmth. She was home.

Much of the story in the first chapter is a combining of the events told to me by my mother, grandmother, great-grandmother, and other relatives. My guess is that the truth lies in all of the recounting, but time and memory – or feelings, which are powerful in coloring 'truth' – skewed the story from one person to the other. By combining them, I thought it would be closer to the truth than choosing one story and writing around my own opinions.

The first three and a half years of Rosebud's life were filled with love and joy. Soon after coming to live with Lillian, she was given her name. Actually, she was given more than one before the dust of the 'name game' had settled. "Naturally, she should be named after me," said Emily. Emily was the family matriarch. In most instances people deferred to her out of respect or fear. Rosebud's first real name was Emily Mary Rose. However, it was not to be the last name for the little Rosebud.

An event that would depose the elder Emily from the power to name, temporarily, happened before the younger Emily's christening day: the Korean War. Though the war was to end the following year, the youngest of Lillian's boys, Bill, was to be shipped out in the days before the christening. It was a tearful time for the family as Bill left. Hugs. Kisses. Crying. Promises. More hugs. Kisses. Crying. Promises. Then, Bill was gone. Everyone met at Lillian's house to wait for the telephone call that Bill had promised to make before departing California for Korea.

The phone rang! Lillian ran to answer it. "Bill, is it you?" she cried. "Ma! Ma! Yeah, it's me. I'm fine. I miss all of you already. I only have a few minutes, so let me speak to sis first." Lillian handed the phone to her younger daughter, Florence. She grabbed the phone from her mother's hand and, in that 50's way, curled the cord around her hand as she began to speak, "Billy, Billy I miss you awfully already. I do hope this terrible war ends tomorrow so you can come back home." The rest of the family waited patiently for their turn, passing the phone from one to the other, and finally it was Lillian's turn again.

She had to say goodbye to her boy, her baby. Now he was a soldier, a man, off to fight for his country. There was so much she wanted to say; but, when she went to speak, Bill began to talk. His words came out in the breathless jumble of youthful excitement, "Mom, sis and I just talked. You just have to, I mean have to, name the baby after sis. Please mom, please. It would mean so much to me for my first niece to have my favorite sister's name. Mom, please, what do you say? Say you will, please! Mom, they're calling me mom, please say yes – mom I have to leave now, please." Of course, Lillian could not refuse her soldier son his last request before he went off to war. So Lillian said, "Yes, Bill, yes. We will name the baby Florence." As he hung up the phone she heard him say, "...and Lillian too, after you." So Emily Mary Rose became Florence Lillian: Florrie, for short.

Florrie had many surprises, far more interesting than a name change, in store for her during her first three years. She began her "education" in earnest with her first trip to England. This happened shortly after her christening. Too young to remember events, she absorbed the essence of her new experiences. Lillian's sister Margaret, and her husband, Gordon, loved the quiet sweet child they knew they would have a responsibility in raising. They did have their own children. The two oldest, girls, were already off on their own. The youngest, a sandy haired seven year old boy named Frankie, was to play a major role in Florrie's life. Mesmerized by the pretty little toddler with dark hair and big blue eyes, Frankie wrapped her tiny fingers around his. He was smitten, and the adults had noticed.

Betrothals were common in the England of days gone by. But in the modern, 1950's England, they still occurred. The family, noticing little Frankie's attraction, agreed that someday Frankie and Florrie would make a fine match. They would be told, when old enough, that the family had made plans for them. In the future, as Florrie grew, she would see Frankie more and more. The family plans for them, sadly, would never materialize. Lives would change forever by events along the way. For now, all there was were dreams for a beautiful future for a young life yet to grow.

Stateside, Florrie's education continued in some very practical ways. The family she had been born into believed that knowledge was the key to success and happiness in life. As an infant, until well past grade school, she was read to every evening by her grandmother, Lillian, or her aunt, Florence. She loved these times. She loved hearing the fairytales with
princesses and princes, castles, magic, and happy endings. Though she did not understand the words at first, she would watch the adults' faces and knew the words meant happy things. Eventually, when

the meanings came, Florrie wanted what these fairytale lives had. She wanted love and happiness forever after.

Her grandfather would take her on his lap every evening and read to her too. His reading was not that of fairytales and happy endings. He read the evening newspaper to her. He knew she didn't understand all of the words. He knew she didn't understand the many important, and the few trivial, stories he would read to her. None of that mattered to him. He wanted her to absorb words, know the mechanics of reading, recognize letters, and develop a love of reading and learning. He was her first teacher. He did his job well. Florrie read at a young age. If it had letters, Florrie wanted to read it. The stories took her away to different lives and different places. Later, she would need to revisit this time to make sense of her world again.

There were lessons about life that Florrie learned too. These lessons began to shape how she viewed the world, her world. Two profound events occurred in Florrie's early years. Lil, her mother, re-appeared ... and she had had a baby. The blonde little infant was Florrie's half-sister, Debbie.

The appearance of her mother was to be the first of many of these appearances and disappearances. Lil drifted in and out of Florrie's life again and again. Sometimes these events occurred as softly as an ebb tide; sometimes they happened with the ferocious roar of a tidal wave.

Lil had her own demons, and they were still chasing her. Florrie would get caught up in this chase again and again. Collateral damage. It would end eventually, but it left a wake of destruction that had caused more damage than meets the eye. Florrie was like a home built on an earthquake damaged foundation; the home would seem safe, but one day an earthquake would come that would cause the already damaged foundation to fail. The house would fall in on itself, destroyed.

This story came from the telling and re-telling of family; it is as was told by all. I learned this story when I was very young. I did not like the story about my name at all. I wanted to be named after my great grandmother. I adored her. I adore her memory now.

When I was with her, there was always magic and never any pain. Though too young to understand it, I felt the pain of my mother's abandonment. It was talked about in hushed whispers and many "too sad's."

I saw hurt in adult eyes and my childish empathy let me feel the pain. Sometimes the pain was more than a little girl should have to bear. My great grandmother, "Mar," lifted me above this pain. She placed me in a land I would grow to love more than I realized at this point in my young life.

England was a land where I could imagine and live without thoughts of being left, abandoned, unwanted. Life takes funny turns sometimes. Even the best of intentions can become poor choices and leave lasting effects. Life taught me that over and over.

CHAPTER THREE – June 1959

Summer again! Florrie loved summers. No school and Frankie too. It was more than she could bear to have Auntie Margaret put her hair in braids that morning. Her aunt, brush moving through Florrie's dark hair, said, "Keep your head still! Oh, you are a flitsy one today, aren't you then?" Florrie was too happy to be still. In a few hours, Frankie would be home from Eton.

She turned and smiled up at her aunt. Her blue eyes, the color of the night sky, seemed to smile too. "Auntie, may I please go to the train station with the driver?" She looked at her aunt wishing to hear the answer she wanted. Sometimes, when she looked up at an adult with her eyes wide and expectant, she thought she could make them do or say whatever she wished. This was one of those times she wished especially hard; but, she knew her Auntie Margaret would never agree to this wish.

"Florrie, you know the driver fetches Frankie from Portsmouth station. It is much too dirty and smoke filled for a young lady. You wouldn't want him to see you in that place, now would you? It will be so much better for him to see you waiting at the door when the car reaches the drive, won't it? That is how proper young ladies behave. There's a good girl. Now go help cook set up the tea. We want it ready before the car leaves."

Obediently, but sadly, Florrie walked to the kitchen and asked the cook how she could help. She was an obedient child, but obedience born of necessity. She was seven now. Last Christmas holiday, back in the states with Granny, Florrie had learned about her mother, learned about abandonment, learned about blame and guilt, and learned that she didn't want anyone to leave her ever again. She was obedient out of fear.3

At her stateside home for that fateful holiday season, Florrie learned more about life than a child her age should have to learn. She had gotten ill almost as quickly as she set foot in the states. This was not unusual. The southern England air agreed with Florrie. It seemed the stateside city air did not. She developed pneumonia. She was asthmatic, and it was not her first bout with pneumonia, so she had a brief hospital stay to be safe.

On the first day out of hospital, at her Granny's house, Florrie settled into her Aunt Flo's big bed with books all around her, dolls around the books, and pictures of Frankie, at Eton on his first day, beyond that. She was tired and weak, but looking forward to Christmas here and then Christmas again in England. Auntie Margaret, Uncle Gordon, and Frankie promised boxes and boxes of Christmas crackers. The big ones with a treat, a toy, a fortune, a motto [joke], and a paper crown.

Florrie loved the paper crowns. She saved them every year and played 'princess' until they fell apart. She would love these Christmas crackers for the rest of her life, and could not have Christmas without them. She saw Auntie Margaret wear a crown, but Auntie Margaret told her it was not a crown. Since only the Queen wore a crown; it was a tiara, and she would have one too someday. Florrie didn't know when someday was, so the paper crowns were perfect for her.

The best part of being sick, Florrie thought, was Granny bringing in her tea. Lillian walked through the bedroom door carrying a beautiful tea tray. She placed the tray on a tea table close to the bed. The teapot had a knitted cozy covering it to help keep the tea warm. Florrie thought about how wonderful the cozy must feel to that teapot. She liked to be wrapped in beautiful scarves when the wind blew so fierce she lost her breath. If she wore a big tea cozy, it would wrap all of her from head to toe! She smiled, snuggled into the fluffy duvet, and settled back against the many pillows she had surrounding her. She wanted to watch the pouring of the tea. It was like a ballet to her.

Florrie watched Lillian carefully as the tea was poured into delicate porcelain cups that rested on matching saucers. Tiny silver spoons lay against the side of each saucer. She would see these same cups years from now, on a kitchen table still in her future, but she would not notice them at that future time.

Carefully, the tea strainer was placed back in its holder. A drop of milk was poured into the fragrant, golden tea. A spoon, never touching the sides of the cups ... nor making a sound ... mingled the transparent and opaque liquids. Ready!

Granny handed her a soft cloth napkin. It was folded into the Prince of Wales feathers. Her favorite! She pulled the two ends and unfurled the creamy white square. Placing it carefully on her lap, she waited for her granny to pass the sugared biscuits. These were always homemade and, if you were lucky, fresh out of the oven and warm. Florrie was lucky that day. Soon the phone would ring and her luck would change; right now, Florrie held a warm sugared biscuit in her hands and savored the sweet smell of the sugar. Nibbling, like a little mouse, she ate half and plated the other half as granny passed her the delicately patterned cup with the warm, soothing, tea.

As Florrie took a small sip of tea, the phone rang. Lillian had placed the phone in the bedroom before the tea service began. She reached for the receiver with a free hand and said hello. It was Lil. Florrie's mother had entered her life once again. This was going to be a tidal wave. Lillian could sense it already. "Yes Lil. I know Lil. No Lil. Yes, of course Lil." Sometimes it was best to just agree with her, thought Lillian.

She could tell from her daughter's voice that she was in no mood to be challenged or talked to, just agreed with and humored. Lillian was glad to oblige. Florrie was leaving for England on Boxing Day, December 26th. Lillian wanted to have nothing but happiness in the house until then, but sometimes we don't get what we want.

Lillian saw Florrie less and less since she and Margaret had agreed, with the help of their mother, Emily, that it would be best if Florrie was educated in England. Emily did not want to see her favorite great grandchild subjected to her eldest grandchild's selfish and cruel ways. She was glad she had formed homes on both sides of the Atlantic. Emily spent most of the year in England, actually following a school calendar, so it was easy for her to bring Florrie with her when she travelled. She was able to spend more time with Florrie, teaching her the proper and ladylike graces she would need. While in the states, Florrie would be surrounded by Emily and her daughter, Lillian. This was the best way to protect this child.

Lillian and Margaret had lived through a horrible war. Both sisters took different views of life away with them. In England, Margaret had married very well. She travelled in high society and royal circles.

The peer title her husband had was just what Margaret had been looking for when choosing a mate.

Her home was small by titled standards, but lavish, and she loved it dearly. It was not a manor house, but it was bright and airy. The gardens, though small too, were beautifully landscaped in the English garden manner. Flowers and shrubs looked like they had grown wild on their own, but it took the gardeners hours to achieve that look. Margaret loved to entertain, and this house was made for it. When not entertaining, Margaret travelled. She had sworn she would never cower in a tube station praying she would not be buried alive by the nasty German bombs. She never cowered to anyone or anything ever again.

Lillian just wanted some happiness. She was afraid in England, though she loved it very much. She was glad when her mother had chosen her and her brother, Charles, to go to America. Margaret, the youngest, and Thomas, the oldest, remained in England. She had found work in a meat packing plant and made a new friend, Henrietta Gick, a German woman! The friendship would last a lifetime. Soon she married. Her aspirations were not as pronounced as her sister's had been. She wanted to find love, have a home, and create a family. Her husband, of British decent, was born in America and had a Native American grandmother. He was wonderful. They had four children. They lived through the depression and hard times with love and hard work. Though always living in apartments that were sometimes too small for the family, they made life work together. They had little, but they had each other. It was all they seemed to need.

Eventually, Thomas came to live in America too, but never Margaret. She would visit, but she would never stay long. Margaret liked being the center of attention. She wanted to be noticed – by every one – everywhere – every time she made an entrance. This was not always the case in America. Her choice of Gordon for a husband had been seriously acted upon once Margaret found out Gordon's family history. The fact he was a Cunard captain and had been an officer in the Royal Navy did not hurt either. Both women had made the right choice for a life partner. Both women helped to shape the attitudes and beliefs of a young Florrie. She would learn to live among the elite with a grace and charm beyond her years. She would learn to exist and survive when she had little left but a will to survive.

"Lil, do you think it's a good idea to speak to her now? She has only been out of the hospital for a few hours. Of course she is your child. No one said she wasn't! No, we are not trying to take her away from you. Don't be silly." Lillian was struggling with her emotions. She knew Florrie was a sensitive child who could pick up on everything around her. However 'adult' this little girl seemed to be, she was still a child and couldn't process all she heard. She held things inside. Sometimes she was so quiet it scared Lillian. Reluctantly, Lillian said quietly to Florrie, "Love, it's your mum. She wants to see how you are feeling. Would you like to tell her? There's a good girl."

Florrie's little outstretched hand grabbed the phone like a lifeline. She did miss mummy sometimes, though she didn't really know her at all. "Hello mummy," Florrie said sweetly. The tide came crashing in.

Lillian watched Florrie's eyes widen as big as saucers. It seemed for a moment that Florrie was one of her dolls that lay scattered about her on the duvet. Then, little lips began to tremble and tears, sparkling and shining like diamonds, fell from the midnight blue eyes like glittering falling stars, and rolled down pale little cheeks to fall on the creamy white napkin that Florrie had placed carefully on her lap moments ago. Lillian did not hear her daughter's words, but she knew they were hurtful. She watched the spirit leave her granddaughter in a few seconds. Lillian approached Florrie on her level, bending down and gently taking the phone from her hand while scooping her other arm around Florrie's now heaving shoulders and pulling her close in a hug. Florrie's little body convulsed with sobs as she held tightly to her Granny. She was trying to stop mummy's words and the mean sound of mummy's voice from echoing in her head. Mean, mean mummy.

The words were hurtful. They were harsh, powerful, and they hurt Florrie in her heart. They cut her as surely as sharp knives. Her love bled out. "You'll do anything for attention, won't you, you stupid little idiot. You just can't stand to see me happy can you? Well, if it weren't for you, my life would be fine.

My life is now hell and it's your fault. I wish you had never been born! What a mistake I made ever having you. You should have died, you fucking little bastard."

"Lil ... Lil ... Lil ...! What are you thinking? Why are you talking to your daughter like that – she's a child, she doesn't understand your problems. Lil had kept on ranting, oblivious that Lillian had taken the phone from her daughter, and she continued to spew poison. Her words were violent and shocking to Lillian. She needed to calm her granddaughter right now. She did not want to be listening to the ravings of this madwoman, her eldest child. She chose her words carefully. She spoke them quietly, but with a firm authority. "Lil, I'm hanging up the phone now. Please do not call back. Do not come near this house. Get help. Until you can be civil to this child, your child, you are no longer part of this family. The receiver only clicked softly as Lillian returned it to its cradle. She would never slam a phone down, no matter how mad she was – and she was madder than she had ever been in her life. The tide receded, taking a little girl's soul with it.

Florrie stood in the doorway of her aunt and uncle's Raynes Road home; she was watching the drive for any sign of the car that would bring Frankie home to her again. The door was slightly ajar so Florrie could hear the clanging and bustling of tea being brought into the beautiful breakfast room that Florrie had helped set up earlier. Suddenly, the car appeared! Florrie called to her aunt and Margaret came outside and walked down the few steps to the drive itself, motioning Florrie to take her place beside her. If Uncle Gordon was home, he would take the first place with Auntie Margaret beside him. Florrie would be relegated to third place. She was glad Uncle Gordon was at sea.

The car pulled to a stop and a valet came out to open the passenger door. Frankie, looking taller than Florrie had remembered, came out of the car smiling. "Hello mum," he said as he kissed his mother's cheeks and then gave her a short and proper English hug. "Hello Florrie," he said as he took Florrie's hand and kissed the top of it softly. Florrie looked from her hand to his eyes, and he winked a sea blue eye at her. "Shall we have our tea ladies?" With those words, Frankie took his mother's arm and Florrie's hand and escorted the two most important women in his life to tea.

The summer went by, as summers must do, too fast for Florrie and Frankie. School would be starting for both of them in a short few days. Frankie's new uniforms and books had already been sent ahead to Eton.

Florrie's school was on the High Street in Fareham, the neighboring town. It was a day school. Margaret and Lillian didn't think Florrie should be sent to a boarding school yet. To the sisters, it seemed like it was the right thing to do, to hold Florrie close for as long as they could.

The memories built that summer would stay with Florrie forever. Frankie took her to magical places. Each day, when they were not busy with visits to even grander homes, horse races where she would curtsy a well-practiced curtsy to a real queen, boat races that were so close to her house she could walk (but Auntie Margaret said that was not proper), and many other things that Auntie Margaret called duties.

Florrie and Frankie would go on many adventures. The beach became a lost island with buried treasure. They would sail, on Frankie's small boat, along the Solent River. Picnics would follow each adventure; when they couldn't eat one more crumb, Frankie would tell stories of Kings and Queens and Princes and Princesses. Florrie would listen to him quietly and intently. She had learned some of these stories in school, but they sounded even more wonderful on days like these. She began to imagine her life in terms of these stories. She had been read to her entire life. She knew many fairy tales. Living here with Uncle Gordon, Auntie Margaret, and her Frankie, Florrie began to equate life with the tales of England's royalty and the fairy tales of childhood.

This is but one of those summers in England. I loved them. It was like living in the fairy tales I had heard so many times. It became an escape for me - the fairy tales – the forays of the summers – hid the pain I knew 'real' life held.

My mother's words had changed me. I do remember that day my mother called. I remember just some of the words – the ones included in this story. There were more of them, then and at other times in my life, when my mother rolled over me like a tidal wave and tried to drag me out to sea. England had become my anchor. I knew I wouldn't drown. I was creating a world where I was safe and in control.

I had a terrible fear of being 'left.' I had a terrible fear of change I didn't know about or see coming. I had a terrible fear of not 'being good' - or, more to the point, good enough.4

I had resolved, at my young age, that I would never lose or relinquish being the 'one in charge.' At almost every tragedy in my family's lives, I took charge – handled things – 'made everything right' again. I grew heady with this power. I believed I was so in control that I was safe... 5

The words my mother said to me that Christmas had another effect as well. I began to dread holidays, Christmas in particular. When they approached, I could feel an ineffable and palpable change in my mind and body. I expected something to go wrong... something bad to happen... I lost my joy in these occasions.

This fear of holidays intensified as I got older, as you will see in my story. Whether self-fulfilling prophesy or ill-timed coincidences, holidays always meant there would be chaos in my life.

Eventually, I began to withdraw from any form of celebrations entirely. If I refused to pay any mind to the occasion, how could I possibly feel any pain? I knew the answer, of course. The pain was IN the withdrawal. I could not find a safe way back.

Then... one Christmas season... a miracle happened. It was this season that had begun the fears, and fitting it would be the season that brought me back from them. I had been watching TV.

Of course, that meant carefully avoiding any holiday programming. But as I scrolled through the channels I heard music... a song... a singer with a rich melodic voice that seemed to draw me through the television screen.

I sat mesmerized. The words touched my heart. The song, "This Christmas Day," was sung by Tommy Farese during a Trans-Siberian Orchestra special. It was a Christmas special that touches my heart like that first time, every time I see it. "She's coming home this Christmas day!"2 I had been 'gone' for so long. It was time for me to come home. Mr. Farese's voice reached my soul when I thought nothing else could. What else could I do...

For the first time in a long time, I put up my tree...

2 Trans-Siberian Orchestra – "Ghosts of Christmas Eve"

CHAPTER FOUR – **December 1969**

Christmas break is a wonderful time until the festivities end and boredom begins. For a high school student, boredom begins about five seconds after the gifts are unwrapped. Flo was bored. No. It was more than simple boredom. She wanted to be back in classes. "God, why are Christmas breaks so long?" Flo had an aversion to holidays that had built steadily since childhood. She whined silently, sighed loudly, rolled her eyes, and hoped to attract the attention of her sister, Debbie. Her sister was still sitting near the Christmas tree. She was surrounded with unwrapped presents and engrossed in conversation with Aunt Florence, Flo's namesake. Debbie would not be easily distracted from being the center of her aunt's attention.

Flo got up from her seat at the once gloriously set dining room table. She picked up a few stacked plates and went a few steps closer to her sister. "Debbie, help me clear this table for granny, please." "That should do it," she thought to herself. Her aunt would think she was behaving 'normally' for once, and her sister, wanting to look good and keep her title as the 'good girl,' would jump at the opportunity to prove her title was just. The sisters, side by side, different as night and day, stacked and carried, cleared and wiped, until the table was empty save for a beautiful centerpiece of pine, berries and holly branches, with taper thin creamy white candles that flickered softly.

"Debbie, don't go in there again! Come into the bedroom and talk to me. I need your advice." "That should get her," Florrie thought. Debbie looked at her sister in wonderment. "This is a first," she thought. She followed Flo into the bedroom they shared and sat on the edge of her twin bed. She waited for her older sister to speak.

Flo was three years older than Debbie. Their lives, though sisters, were dramatically different. Debbie, raised by Lillian from age seven, was protected and sheltered, especially by Aunt Florence. Flo, who was raised between two continents, considered herself worldly and an adult. When she was in third grade, Flo left England, her Auntie Margaret and Uncle Gordon, and Frankie. There was trouble at home in the states. Her godparents, Aunt Florence and Uncle Tommy, were divorcing. The family was in the midst of moving to Staten Island. It was time to leave the railroad flat they had called home. It was a change precipitated by family trouble, but looked upon as a good change for the sake of the two young girls who were soon to become young women. For the most part, the change was a good one.

England was a memory for Flo now. A place, once called home, became a place one occasionally visited. Lately, Flo had been too busy with her friends to take a summer abroad. She retained her time-clouded memories of England, and the knowledge that Frankie would probably become her husband one day, but 'real' life had begun to intrude again, even here.

"Debbie, you have to help me!" Flo looked at her sister with the saddest face she could muster. She was sad. She wanted help, but she wanted to manipulate her sister into asking if she could help - do her a favor. Flo would have done anything to make her sister comply; Flo did not want to ask for the favor outright. "What is it? Is something wrong? Did something happen?" Debbie questioned her sister for specifics, particulars. Flo obliged.

Flo knew who he was, but was always afraid to talk to him. He captained the football team. He was tall, dark, and handsome. All the girls fainted [or giggled convulsively] at the sight of him. Then, one day, just before the holiday break, it happened. Flo was standing at her locker during a class change. The halls were crowded, as usual. Sounds of laughter and happiness echoed through the cavernous hallways of Curtis High School in Staten Island. Lockers opened and slammed. It was the day before Christmas break and everyone was happy and in a holiday rush. Teachers were pleasant. Voices had an almost musical lilt. Even the usual cacophonous sounds were soothing and melodic. Caught up in the sounds and in the thoughts in her head, Flo didn't see him approach. There was a soft tapping on her shoulder and she turned. --- It was him!

The world seemed to stop on its axis. Leonard Jerome Anderson Jr., captain of the football team, hunk, dreamboat, stud, cutie, hot, and magnificent – was standing in front of her in all his glory. Flo was speechless as she looked up into his dark, dreamy, bedroom eyes. The noises that had just lulled her into a paralyzing complacency were silent now. Flo heard nothing. She saw nothing but the vision standing, smiling handsomely, before her.

When she could hear once again, Flo heard a voice. It was a mix of Brooklyn and Italian with some recent Staten Island thrown casually in for effect. She realized the voice came from this vision of a young man standing before her. He was also laughing, a soft and charismatic laugh that made Flo draw in an audible breath before her mind returned to the real and noisy hallway of Curtis High School. "Hey, I didn't mean to scare you, babe." Len said smiling. He was leaning against the next locker. As he spoke, he reached up to swipe a lock of Flo's hair away from her face. "I said, do you want to get together for a movie or something during break?"

Flo looked into his eyes. Her heart was in her throat. How the hell was she going to speak – coherently? She wanted time to stop. How did this happen? How, why, did he notice her? He could, and often did, have any girl he wanted. He was standing here, by her locker, talking to her, and asking her out...on a date...oh God.

She turned back to her locker. A stack of books, still piled in her arms, had begun to feel heavy. She struggled to push them into the locker. Len effortlessly pushed himself from the neighboring locker and scooped the books up in one hand. He angled them into the locker in a split second move, and they lay neatly in the locker bottom. With the same hand, he lifted Flo's chin until she had no choice but to look into those wonderful bedroom eyes once more. "Now, are you going to say yes?" Knowing there was no other answer possible, Flo said "yes."

"He gave me his number and now I have to call him. Call him! How can I do that? What will I say?" Flo was pacing as she spoke, and Debbie was swaying her head back and forth like she was watching a particularly enthusiastic match at Wimbledon. She knew her sister was excited. She knew what this meant for her; there would be no rest until her sister had taken control of the situation. No, more than just control; Flo would need to master every aspect of this simple request for a phone call and a date. She knew her sister needed to analyze and predict every situation. Nothing was ever just what it was for Flo. She knew what Flo wanted. Flo wanted a way to see if this was real or a joke without getting hurt. Flo wasn't sure why Len asked her out. Maybe one of his team mates dared him to do it. Maybe he dumped his current girlfriend, and her sister was the first girl he saw afterward. Maybe he just liked her. Flo would have to know why before she could feel safe.

"What if I called him?" Debbie said quietly. "You!" exclaimed Flo. "What would you say to him?" she questioned. "Well, I could say that you've been doing nothing but talking about him since break began. I could say that you were shy and didn't want to call him until near the end of break in case he was busy with his family. I could ask him to call you so I can have some peace," Debbie said seriously. "Oh, Deb; you are the best sister in the world," Flo said honestly as she threw her arms around her sister in a rare display of true sisterly affection.

Debbie did call Len. Len did call me. It wasn't too long before I asked my family to break my betrothal to my cousin Frank. He was now in the Royal Navy and came to see me on shore leave. I told him about Len. He graciously released me from our promise. It broke his heart, but I did not know that then. I don't think I would have cared. I knew only that I loved Len.

We married after a stormy engagement. It was an appropriate foreshadowing of a marriage from hell.

Len was an alcoholic. He was when I met him. I knew. His friends, and yes, his family, told me. I thought I could change him. I thought I was in control. I thought love was enough. I thought and thought and thought...but, I did not 'see.' The drinking became progressively worse. It was followed by more of the verbal abuse I had now become used to. The physical abuse began before our son, Lenny, was born. It became worse much quicker than the verbal abuse did. Soon, our daughter Amy was born. I had been raised in an atmosphere with a respect for marriage. I had seen what happened when my Aunt Flo divorced my Uncle Tom. I adored my uncle, but I never saw him again. Marriage makes people leave. No one ever told me the hell that happens when people stay.

CHAPTER FIVE – **March 1979**

Amy's Story

Mornings seemed to come too fast that week, the last week of her daughter's life. Flo would reflect on that simple fact much later. Now, at this moment, Flo thought March was a cold, gray month even without the added burden of very early mornings. It was Saturday. Cleaning and shopping would be her priority. Still in a warm bed, Flo heard the sound of the coyote falling off that same cliff for the millionth time and knew her son was awake and watching "The Road Runner" cartoons. Grabbing a robe, she reluctantly slid from her warm bed, shuffled into her slippers, and walked sleepily to the stairs. A movement from her daughter's bedroom caught her eye, and Flo stopped and went inside.

The room was pink. Amy loved pink. The furniture was a soft, creamy white with gold-leafed accents. The bed was canopied with yards of cotton candy sheer fabric, embroidered with daisies, flowing from a center crown and dripping down all four sides. It was a room fit for a princess. Amy was sitting in the middle of her bed. The flannel nightgown, pink and soft, skimmed her tiny body and melted into the bedclothes.

She was rubbing her eyes with small clenched fists. Her words were almost a whisper, "Mommy, Lenny woke me up and I'm still tired. Can I go back to sleep?"

Even when tired, she spoke with the soft, lilting voice of an angel. Amy looked at Flo with sleepy, crystal blue eyes, and Flo smiled. Her sandy blonde hair, mussed from a night of sleep, was a tumble of curls.

Anyone who looked at Amy smiled. Her husband said that when Amy looked at you, you were touched by love. Smiles always followed this little one. Flo went to the bed and softly laid Amy's head back down on the pillow. She pulled the soft pink and white duvet up to Amy's chin and kissed the top of the tumble of sandy blonde curls. She paused for a moment to inhale the soft, sweet scent of her child. The scent reminded Flo of baby powder and field flowers; it was comforting and sweet. Amy always played with flowers. She had them placed in small vases and jars all around the house. Every time she passed a vase she would inhale and a smile would form on her face. "Go back to sleep for a little while, Tickenpuck," Flo quietly whispered. Turning back to the stairs, Flo glanced one more time at her now sleeping daughter. She headed down the stairs.

In the bay windowed living room, the television drowned out the sound of Lenny playing with his favorite matchbox cars. Flo yelled, "Turn that down, Nuk! Are you deaf? You know you woke your sister, don't you?" As she walked into the room, she lowered the volume on the blaring TV set. Lenny kept on making his engine sounds as one car inevitably crashed into another, and Flo headed into the kitchen to begin breakfast.

After breakfast, as Flo did the breakfast dishes, she listened to the sounds of Jerry Mouse trying desperately to avoid confrontation with Tom Cat. Her son and the Saturday morning cartoons were a team, like bagels and cream cheese or peanut butter and jelly; they went together.

She thought about Amy, sleeping in her pink princess bedroom, and decided that her daughter had been sleeping long enough. As Flo walked up the stairs to Amy's room, a chill came over her. She turned and looked down the stairs at the front door to the house. She was standing on the middle of the stairway, one hand on the railing. "Funny," she thought, as she began shivering. She was so cold she had thought someone had opened the door and let in the March wind. She turned, shaking her head, and continued up the stairs. She entered Amy's room, still shivering, with her arms hugging her body.

Amy was lying on her side facing the door. Flo stopped for a moment to look at her. What a beautiful little angel she was lying there. Her arm stuck out from under the covers and rested next to her face. The small fingers curled gently. Amy was a beauty at six years old. Petite in form and features, sandy blonde hair streaked with gold from the sun, eyes that were the color of the sky on a sunny summer day, lips and cheeks as pink as a fresh-bloomed rose, Amy looked like an angel to Flo.

Placing her finger in Amy's hand, Flo felt the warmth and softness only a child has. She moved her child's hand and gently reached for the small shoulder near to it. "Amy. Honey, it's time to wake up," she whispered softly as she gently shook her daughter's shoulder. Nothing! She shook harder this time. "Amy, do you hear mommy?" A slow movement came from the small form under the covers and Flo felt her breath release.

She thought for a second about the panic she had just felt at such a common thing as a child not waking at the first call. Maybe she was still spooked by the cold rush of air in the stairway? Flo dismissed it from her mind... for now. She helped Amy out of bed and, with a soft little hand ensconced in hers, mother and daughter walked slowly down the stairs to the living room. When she reached the couch, Amy lay down once again. Flo went back upstairs to make the beds and get dressed. She still felt cold.

Time for you to get dressed, Lenny," Flo called as, once again, she ran down the stairs. "You had better be a good boy today because Daddy's coming home." Living in Pennsylvania and having a husband who worked in New York City was hard on a marriage. Their marriage had been showing signs of strain long before the decision to move to Pennsylvania. The times Flo came home to a very drunk husband were many. The abuse didn't always need the fuel of alcohol, imagined jealousy ignited it too. He was always sorry afterward, but distancing in both their hearts had happened. Both thought the move would help. It had ... at first.

Now, Flo found she was home alone with the children more and more often. There always seemed to be an excuse why Len could not make it home. There had been times when he had not come home for weeks.

When...if... Len came home tonight; Flo hoped they were going to have a talk. They were now at the breaking point. She knew she needed to leave him, but she was afraid of what he would do. His violence, his rage, when released, was capable of anything – anything at all.6

Rounding the corner of the living room and glaring at her seven-year-old son, still in front of the television set, she saw Amy lying motionless on the couch. Flo went to her and shook her by the small, flannel ensconced shoulders. Amy's eyes flew open. The crystal blue eyes were staring straight ahead and Flo could see that the pupils of Amy's eyes were dilated. Something was wrong! What was happening?

Flo wanted to scream. "Come on," she thought to herself, "think clearly and you'll get through this. Don't alarm Lenny. Dear God, what do I do?" Flo's grandmother, Lillian, lived next door. Flo's sister, Debbie, was staying there until summer. She needed to get to them right away. "Lenny, watch the cartoons for a few more minutes while Mommy runs over to Granny's house," she spoke softly, but her voice seemed to echo in her ears.

She got up slowly and forced herself to walk calmly to the door. Once outside she bolted to her grandmother's door and ran inside.

Lillian and Debbie were sitting at the kitchen table deep in conversation. Both were very good at verbalizing. Morning tea had just been finished. The usual 'Brown Betty' tea pot was on side of the kitchen table. Porcelain tea cups, the ones from years ago, stood half empty of the smoky amber tea. Tiny teaspoons rested gently on the saucers.

Crumbs from the scones, no doubt baked fresh that morning, were haphazard on the linen tablecloth. Strawberry jam, lidless, probably her sister's doing, sat red and fragrant on the center of the table alongside empty bowls that once held mounds of rich clotted cream.

Flo stood wild-eyed in the kitchen doorway, amazed she had actually gotten this far, and the chattering stopped. "What's wrong?" Debbie questioned Flo as she quickly got up from the well-worn kitchen chair and started walking toward her, arms outstretched. "It's Amy," croaked Flo, surprised that she had managed to find her voice. "Something is wrong with her. She won't wake up. I think it may be some kind of coma. Her pupils are dilated. She didn't recognize me! Come and look at her. Now! Please!"

Debbie and Flo were out the door as they spoke. Lillian followed right behind them; her eyes, pale blue, looked frightened. She knew what she would see. Lillian had seen the shadow of death in people's faces before; they all died. The three women covered the distance between the two homes in seconds that seemed like hours.

They were huddled around Amy's small, still form. All of them were looking at her. Time seemed to stop. Flo's mind drifted back to bath time a week ago. She remembered carrying Amy's wet little towel-wrapped body from the bathtub to her bed. She remembered nuzzling the bubble bath sweet, wet, warm skin of her little girl. She remembered thinking how lucky she was to have these two beautiful children.

She knew she would die if anything ever happened to them. She remembered her daughter's words to her that night. "Mommy, I'm going to die. I have to talk to Jesus and the only way I can do that is if I die. There's something I know I have to do and Jesus will help me. He promised He would. I want to be buried in the cemetery next to Great-grandma Mar." Flo remember thinking it was just child's talk. "Dear God! It was true! My little girl knew she was going to die, and she was trying to prepare me for her death," the thought stunned her. Amy was always religious. Church was a haven for her. Flo had always questioned faith. Belief was not easy for her. It would never be easy for her.

The drive to the hospital seemed to take forever. The misty cold rain turned slowly to sleet as the car made its way from the small country town, to the double lane highway, to the small town hospital over twenty minutes away on a good day. Debbie was driving and Flo, in the back seat, held Amy's quiet little body tightly against her. Mother and daughter locked together, hearts beating in unison, for what was to be the last time.

Flo thought about Lenny at home with her grandmother and hoped that they didn't upset him leaving in the mad rush that they did. Cradling Amy's head against her shoulder, Flo started to talk to her daughter. "It's all right, my little angel. Mommy knows you will be better soon." She tried to sound reassuring to Amy and her sister, but she knew Amy was dying. Amy had told her she would. Amy never lied.

The Emergency Room staff rushed them into a room as soon as they walked through the ER door. Nurses began to swarm over the tiny body like bees drawn to a flower. The best pediatrician in the area was in the hospital that morning. The on-call doctor in the emergency room paged him as soon as he looked at Amy. The pediatrician was a large and friendly looking young man. His bushy dark hair and big brown eyes enhanced his friendly look. He would, just by his presence, make a child feel at ease. He looked like a big friendly puppy. His concern about this tiny little patient deepened the lines above his brows, and he frowned. He talked quietly, but urgently to his staff.

It didn't take a medical degree to figure out the look on the faces of the people who examined her daughter. Flo stood there watching them scurry around Amy, her little angel, lying so still on the exam table. As another nurse came in to start a second I. V. on Amy, the doctor took Flo to the other side of the room. He put his hands on the top of Flo's shoulders and looked her in the eyes. He began to speak, "Your daughter has a rare condition called Reyes Syndrome.[7]

You said your whole family is just getting over the flu. All we know about Reyes is that it's brought on by viral illnesses in children. The disease progresses in stages. Survival depends on how quickly these stages develop. Your little girl is in the third stage of the disease already. You should prepare yourself and your family for your daughter's death.

There isn't much we can do here so we're transferring her, by ambulance, to Geisinger Medical Center in Danville.[8] You can ride in the ambulance with her. I'm sorry to be so abrupt, but time is critical here."

As the doctor stopped talking, he kept his comforting hands on Flo's shoulders, waiting for the inevitable reaction. Flo's body began to sink. Her knees seemed unable to hold her up any longer. The doctor steadied her gently. He knew this reaction would happen. He had delivered many similar messages before. Flo went numb. She looked at her precious little girl knowing that she would not be able to look at her much longer. She braced herself, shook off the doctor's hands, and walked to her child.

The nurses were already starting to prepare Amy for the long ambulance ride. Flo thought about her decision not to be vaccinated for the flu this year. She wouldn't let her children get the shot either. After all, hadn't that news show said flu shots might be dangerous?9 Now, God ... now, what could be more dangerous than this?

The sleet had turned to a heavy snow by the time they began the two hour ride to the next hospital. The ambulance crew was not only concerned for this precious cargo, but for the terrible and deteriorating weather conditions as well. The ride was filled with slides and spins on the barely drivable roads. Flo kept holding Amy's hand and talking, oblivious to the weather – oblivious to everything but her little girl.

"My little angel, my love, please don't leave mommy. You have to get better for all of us Ticken. What will I do without you? Come on baby, please try for mommy. I love you so much." Flo took her free hand and gently stroked he daughter's temple, wiping away a stray sandy blonde curl. It was the same curl she had brushed from her daughter's eyes this morning.

Much later, Flo was staring at the floor in the waiting room of the pediatric intensive care unit at the medical center for what seemed like hours. A nurse, with a caring smile, told her that she could see her daughter after she was set up in her room.

Flo had called her husband, who was still at work in the city, before she had left in the ambulance. He was on his way. While waiting to see her child, she called her family and told them all she knew so far. All that was left to do now was to wait. Amy would miss so much of life. Flo would never see what kind of woman Amy would become. She would never see Amy's wedding day. She would never see Amy's babies, now forever unknown grandchildren. How could she possibly get through this?

Flo looked up to see the nurse calling her from the door of her daughter's room. She stood slowly, making sure her knees, which had felt like jelly since the emergency room, and wanted nothing more than to let her sink to the floor, would hold her weight. Sure she could stand up without worry, Flo allowed the waiting nurse to escort her into Amy' new bedroom, a bedroom without the trappings of a princess, a bedroom cold, sterile, and without the smell of flowers.

Later that night, Flo and her husband, who had indeed arrived at the hospital, made the long drive home after the doctors told them there was nothing they could do except get a good night's rest. Assured that someone would be calling them if there was a change in Amy's condition, they reluctantly agreed to leave.

Flo wanted to stay in the hospital. Knowing she could see her daughter, even for a brief five minutes every hour, was comforting to her.

Lenny was tired from working and driving and wanted to get some sleep. She knew he would want to go home. She didn't know what would release his anger anymore. It was easier to give in to him, especially now. She was frantic in her mind about Amy. One thing at a time, she thought. They went home.

When the phone rang Sunday morning, Flo knew it was bad news. The voice on the phone sounded hollow in her ears, "Amy has gone into cardiac arrest. She is stable, but we need you to come back to the hospital as soon as you can. You should know that Amy is now hooked up to a respirator." The doctor had told her that Amy wasn't breathing enough on her own to sustain life. She held the phone against her chest, swaying slowly, until Len took it from her hand and helped her up the stairs. She and Len got ready for the long ride back to the hospital.
Nothing in the world can prepare you for the sight of seeing a child so utterly helpless. The tubing, the wires, the sounds are frightening. When it's your child, the sight is indescribable. The feelings are ineffable. Flo and Len clung to each other, staring in disbelief at the tiny form of their daughter's body, now overwhelmed by the insidious machines. The respirator hissed as Amy's little chest expanded, in a fake sort of way, under the pressure of the life giving oxygen. The heart monitor's steady, rhythmic beats echoed in the bright, sterile room. The smells of alcohol and antiseptic flew through the air. How long could they endure this horror?

Flo reached through wires and tubes to touch a small, soft spot on Amy's hand. It was below one of the many IV's, with colored liquids streaming down hollow tubes, snaked into her daughter's arms. She felt the smooth, warm skin under her fingertips. "Please God!" she softly whispered as tears fell down her cheeks.

By late afternoon, both Flo and Len were exhausted. The doctors had advised Flo that she could lie down across the hall in the bed that the on call doctors use at night. She did lie down while Len sat in the hall drinking cups of coffee. Then, the awful noise of a heart monitor suddenly flat lining could be heard. The sound was piercing. It pierced Flo's heart for sure. Another cardiac arrest!

Flo knew it was Amy, but she couldn't move from the bed. Her body would not respond. Every fiber of her being was paralyzed by the shrill, screeching sound. She lay there counting the minutes. It was just over six minutes when she heard the sound finally end. She knew that amount of time meant brain death. Her body released. Finding her movement and steadying herself on her feet, she pulled herself up from the bed, and ran into the hall.

The doctor was coming out of Amy's room and beginning to talk to Len. Flo flew at the doctor and started to pound on his chest with clenched and shaking fists. She was screaming words, but incoherent. Len and other nurses and doctors pulled her, so very gently, from him. A stretcher seemed to materialize out of nowhere, and Flo felt her body being placed on it and strapped down. The sting of a needle in the crook of her elbow and a blessed wave of dreamless sleep washed over her. She was taken to the Emergency Room and sedated again. Blissful nothingness enveloped her...and she smelled the sweet smell of flowers.

Later, in Amy's room again, Flo apologized to everyone. They had understood. She would come to know that they had seen this kind of reaction before; her actions did not shock or surprise them. Len had already shown Flo the EKG strip from Amy's cardiac monitor. They had a major decision to make.

Seeing their daughter on Monday morning decided for them. Amy was brain dead. Her beautiful little body had started to deform. Her arms and legs began to pull up and bend. Her hands began a process called flexion, where the hands twist backwards and begin to curl. Caring nurses told them it was the body reverting to the position it had in the womb.

Because of her slowing circulation, blood pooled at her back. It was stained purple, the color of the grape jam in Amy's favorite peanut butter and jelly sandwiches, in stark contrast to the rest of Amy's pale porcelain skin. They couldn't stand to see her that way. Their beautiful little girl was no longer there with them. They held each other and cried.

The doctor walked into the waiting room and sat with Amy's parents. With him, a group of doctors, administrators, and lawyers stood quietly and somberly. Everyone was silent. Len spoke first, "We know that there is no hope of Amy ever coming out of the coma. You told us yesterday that she would probably live just a few weeks longer on the machines ... then ... well ... another major cardiac arrest would stop her heart for good. We were wondering if it would be possible to disconnect her respirator. Looking at her just lying there, we can't take it anymore. My wife is falling apart." Len couldn't speak anymore. Flo looked at her husband through her tears. She could see that he was crying too.

The doctor told them the reason that he and the others were there was to discuss that specific option. Now that they had made their feelings clear, they would go ahead with the process necessary to disconnect the respirator. This was Monday morning, and the process would take two days. There was procedure to follow. There were legalities to work out.

Wednesday morning was cold and snowy. It was a gray day for a gray mood. Flo found it hard to look at Amy that day. Standing by Amy's bedside, Flo and Len were silent. The five minutes of visiting time that were allowed every hour seemed to go so fast. Flo's mind raced with thoughts: "Could we allow this to happen? Would one of us change our minds? I wish they would let us stay with her until it was time. Dear God, it feels like an execution!"

When it was time, Flo sat across the hall in the waiting room. Len requested to be with Amy, but Flo couldn't. She couldn't watch her daughter die. She had given Amy life and watched her take her first breath, but she would not watch her take her last breath. It seemed like an eternity later when Len came back into the waiting room. "It's over. Amy's gone." He said with tears streaming down his face.

In their grief, Amy's parents clung to each other. They cried as the sounds of the hospital washed over them. Together, they walked to Amy's bedside to say their last goodbye.

"Yes, Amy, you can go back to sleep." ~ Mommy

Reyes Syndrome is a disease that most often attacks the liver and brain. It is thought to occur after beginning to recover from a viral illness. It occurs, therefore, most frequently during flu season. Commonly, it also occurs during outbreaks of chicken pox, though Reyes Syndrome can strike anytime. If not treated very early, it is most often fatal. Though treated, it may still have a fatal outcome. Those who do recover are likely to suffer profound mental retardation. There are few who come through unscathed. It is difficult to diagnose because it resembles many other illnesses. Symptoms usually are vomiting, fatigue, and drowsiness in the early stages. This stage, however, progresses rapidly to disorientation, combativeness, confusion, delirium and/or convulsions, and coma. Many emergency room physicians, who have not had experience with Reyes Syndrome, may misdiagnose it. (NRSF Information)

KAREN ANN QUINLAN

Had it not been for a prior case law, Flo and Len would not have had the ability to end their daughter's pain and suffering.

This prior case was that of a young woman, Karen Ann Quinlan. In the spring of 1975, Karen's parents received the phone call most parents dread. She had mixed alcohol and pills. Karen was in the hospital and had slipped into a coma. Within days, the coma was deemed irreversible. Karen's body began to contort. Her parents wanted to end her pain, but they had to petition the courts because the hospital would not follow their wishes. They won the right to disconnect Karen from the machines in the spring of 1976. (Quinlan History)

Karen's brave family had paved the way for Flo and her husband to let their daughter rest in peace.

In Memory of My Daughter

In the quiet of the night,
I sit alone.
So many thoughts run through my mind...
Fast forward, and then reverse
Never-ending.
I close my eyes.
I shake my head, trying to pull a single thought... from memory.
From the jumble –
But I fail.
They come ... all at once ...
In a giant tidal wave of thoughts,
rolling in, ebb tide unbounded.
Finally, as my mind reaches an overloaded exhaustion,
- one thought comes –

An ineffable sadness washes my soul in salty tears.
I don't want this memory, this pain, but it comes.
It floats easily out of the many.
It always reaches me first.

... Amy.

CHAPTER SIX – **May 1980**

Early on that beautiful May morning there was a knock on her front door. Flo had just fallen into a restless sleep. Her sleep had been restless since that cold day in March when her beautiful little girl, Amy, died. She had no power over that, no control, so, in the days following her daughter's death, she strove to regain the one coping mechanism she knew – her control. Throughout her daughter's funeral she was driven to control every aspect of the wake and burial. It consumed her. She planned what her daughter would wear. She planned what would be in the casket. She planned what jewelry would be appropriate for her little girl to wear. She planned what everyone would be allowed to wear to the funeral. She planned what behavior would be acceptable for 'guests.' She planned to keep her sanity.

Much had happened during the year since her daughter's death. She had come to the painful realization that her marriage was over. Flo had known this long before Amy's death, but she would not see it or address it if she did. It would mean she had no control. Flo would never admit to losing the one thing she had clung to through all the ups and downs in her life so far. It was the one thing she had fought so hard to get back when Amy died. But, one night the realization presented itself to her, and she could not deny it any longer.

On the night Flo realized the need to accept the death of her marriage, Len came home drunk. This was not surprising to Flo. He had been a drinker when they met. She had been warned. She had turned a deaf ear and a blind eye. She had believed that she could 'fix' Len; she believed she could change him. She thought that her love could make miracles possible. She assumed this was in her control. She was wrong. She just didn't know how wrong she was ... yet.

There had been a progression to his drinking and his behavior. At first, though he drank rarely, he binged. Once he had one drink, he had to drink himself into oblivion. There was no such thing as a casual or social drink with Len. Eventually, his drinking became more and more frequent. It took greater amounts of alcohol to send him into the unconscious stupor he craved. Because he could drink longer, drink more, his behavior when drunk escalated. He had always been a mean drunk. Now he was an abusive mean drunk. His anger, once unleashed, was so swift, so violent, and so consuming, that Flo began to walk on eggshells around him.

She almost left after Amy was buried. It was a difficult time for all of the family. It was a heartbreakingly difficult time for Flo. She rarely left the house. Sometimes she rarely left Amy's bedroom. She could still smell the sweet floral and powder scent of her child.

Three days after Amy was buried next to her great-grandmother in the small church cemetery that Amy loved so much, Flo suffered another loss. Rebel, the family dog, Amy's dog really, died. He was two and a half years old. The vet said he died of a broken heart. Flo knew this was possible. She was dying of a broken heart too, but not quickly enough.

A few weeks after that cold and blustery day when she watched her only daughter lowered into cold dark nothingness, Len actually began to worry about Flo. He asked some friends for help. It was decided that they would take Flo to a local bar/restaurant for a drink and dinner. These friends were drinking buddies of Len's, and the restaurant part of the establishment was iffy at best. Flo agreed, reluctantly, when they said she could leave at any time.

Sitting at the bar, Flo stared at the drink in front of her and twirled the daisy she had in her hand. It was one of Amy's daisies. She looked at Len and his friends. Laughter, and the loose talk of a few drinks downed, echoed around them. Flo felt invisible. She wanted to be. Life held no meaning for her yet. She had not found her will to go on with the business of living. She was about to begin her journey back any second now... listen: "Len, I want to go home."

The change was sudden and frightening. Gone were the smiles and laughter. Flo, at that moment, understood what she had not wished to see for all these years: she could not change Len. The realization that she did not want to any longer did come as a surprise to her though. Her love for him had died long ago. Flo had walled that realization away. It was no longer contained now. Funny, she thought, this awareness gave her strength. She turned to face Len and, quite calmly, said "I want to go home – now – please."

Len looked at her with rage in his eyes. His body began shaking as he searched for words to spit at his wife. She had gone against him in public. She had challenged him. This had not happened in a long time. He had thought he had beaten this obstinacy out of her. The thought of having to beat this attitude out of his wife again aroused him, and in this excitement he found his voice. "If you think I'm letting your dead daughter stop me from enjoying a night out with my friends, you have got to be crazier than I thought you were. You sit your ass in a chair and shut the fuck up until I say I'm ready to leave, you fucking cunt." The words flew from between lips dotted with froth and spittle. He looked rabid. Flo was afraid, but would not back down. "Take me home right now, or I will walk. Your choice. Decide." Flo said this with more conviction than she actually felt, but it empowered her like nothing else had in a long time.

Len did bring Flo home that night. He left and went right back to the bar. When he did come back home, the beating was inevitable. The next morning, Flo told him she wanted to leave. He begged her not to go. Flo didn't know where to go if she did leave. Len was such a charmer that her family loved him still. She had protected him. Her family did not know the real demons buried deep inside her husband. She didn't really know all of them either. She had seen some of them though – many, many times. She stayed, yet again – but not for long.

That final death throe of the marriage came on another night a few weeks later when Len came home drunk. It was, as said earlier, a usual thing for Len to come home drunk. What made this night different was where he had chosen to 'put' Flo after the usual beating. She was at the sink when he came in the door. The final dish was washed and rinsed and still in her hand. "Where the hell is dinner?" He screamed slurred words at her.

Flo knew always to have a plate of food to warm, no matter the time of day. "I'll heat it up now Len." She turned to open the refrigerator and Len pounced like a lion on the weakest of the herd. She didn't feel the first blow. The shock of the attack gave her a moment's reprieve from the pain. Soon, though, the blows were reigning down on her, and all she could do was cower in a fetal position and try to protect herself from serious damage.

When he was tired, he stopped as suddenly as he began. He grabbed the hair on the top of her head and pulled her up from the floor. The pantry door was ajar and he pulled it open and threw Flo into the tiny, cramped space. The door slammed hard behind her, and the rain of knives, from a holder behind the pantry door, began to fall.

Flo lost track of time. She didn't know how long she stayed in that pantry, crouched on the tiny open space on the floor. She didn't know how many knives fell from the full rack. She didn't know how many cut and pierced her skin as they fell. She smelled the copper tinged scent of blood – her blood. But she could not risk moving. She could not risk making a sound. She could not risk being beaten again.

When Flo could no longer hear sounds beyond the door, she opened it slowly and quietly. The light of the kitchen hurt her eyes. Squinting, she could see Len sitting at the kitchen table. His head slumped on the placemat before him. He had passed out. Flo crawled on her hands and knees from the pantry to the sink. She sat on the ground and looked over her world and she cried.

Knives, scattered on the floor inside and around the pantry, glistened in the light. Blood was streaked where Flo had crawled from the womb of the tiny pantry. Born again, Flo looked at the knives – then she looked at Len. She would end this now.

She pulled herself up, using the sink for balance; she stood and looked at the rack where the knives used to be. Slowly, she walked to the first knife and picked it up. She placed it, very gently, in the rack. Then a second, a third...and she stopped. The largest knife was at her feet. She bent and picked it up.

She looked at her reflection in the blade. She was unrecognizable to her own eyes. She turned to look at the passed out drunk at her kitchen table. She walked up to the chair. His back was to her; he was lost in a world of his alcoholic demons. Flo raised the knife and steadied the blade with both hands wrapped tightly around the hilt; she was ready to plunge it deeply into the cause of her pain. She looked up and froze. There was her son in his pajamas, looking at her with his blue eyes opened wide!

Flo maintained eye contact with her son as she said, "Len, go upstairs and get one favorite toy and your BARE bear. Mommy is cleaning the kitchen and we are going on a vacation! Go on then, be a good boy." Little feet pounded up the steps and a toy box opened loudly. Flo put the knife down next to her husband's head. She wanted him to understand what almost happened that night. She grabbed her son and, together, they left in the night.

Another death had occurred in Flo's life. A marriage died. There would be more....

The pounding on the door would not go away. Flo got out of bed and went to the door. She pulled it open and there stood three police officers, hats in hand. She knew. Flo had expected this day since she met Len all those years ago. Sometimes, she even prayed for it.

Flo had gone to pick up her son. Len had had him for the weekend. He had told her to stay. It was a long drive back to Staten Island, where Flo now lived once again, from the Poconos. He had to go pick up his newly chromed Dharma Ducati – Desiree. He would be testing her into the night. She agreed. She even offered to make dinner. Lenny was watching cartoons. She was cooking. Len was reading the paper. Why couldn't her marriage have been like this? Flo made pork chops. They were Len's favorite. The three of them sat at the kitchen table, alcohol free, and had dinner, together. Len helped her clear the table and said he would leave soon. He told her he would sleep on the couch if he did come home early. The divorce papers had been signed a week ago. She knew he would not invade her space. He went to the refrigerator and pulled a beer from the shelf.

"Len!" Flo cautioned. "You are going to be riding a motorcycle tonight. Please, don't drink that." Opened as soon as it met his hand, Len offered Flo the beer. "You have it then, okay?" She took it and smiled at him. He left to fetch Desiree.

Everyone knew this would be the way Len would meet his end – an early end. Last week he had turned twenty nine. He would never see thirty. The police had told Flo all they knew. The investigation was still ongoing. They would not have come as quickly as they did, but the accident had happened across the street from the funeral home Amy had been waked from a year ago. The funeral director told them where Len lived. Fate had put Flo there to receive the news.

Len had gone to the bars after picking up his motorcycle that night. He had been so drunk he could not sit on a bar stool. He hit the tree at 120 mph. Death was instantaneous. A full helmet, which Len always wore, could not handle an impact like that. His face, and all behind it, had been pushed into his chest cavity. His funeral would be a closed casket. Flo thought about Lenny, still asleep in his bed. How could she tell him this so soon after his sister had died? She asked the police to accompany her upstairs. Lenny's first question was: "Was my daddy drunk?"

It was almost a relief to me when Len died. He was sweet that last evening, but that was an exception. Len did not stop beating me when I left him. His cruelty was as evil as his sweetness was good. I wish he could have been helped, but he died the way he always knew he would. Sometimes I think it was a relief to him too. I know Lenny and I could breathe easier afterward. He was not only abusive to me. The children had suffered too. Why didn't I leave sooner? I don't know. Part of me still wanted to believe I could save him. I didn't think I could survive on my own. I thought he would kill me if I left. I think he would have eventually..... though I'm sure he would have felt bad when he sobered up.

CHAPTER SEVEN – **January 1987**

"The news isn't good angel."

Flo heard her mother speak the words she had known would come again since the day seven years ago when she had heard them the first time. Flo had just begun to trust the bond she and her mom had formed. It was hard work, and at one point, seemed impossible. The years of coming in and out of Flo's life seemed to have severed that parental bond, but both had worked to become civil. When Amy and Len had died, both had begun speaking regularly until her mother had her first cancer diagnosis.

Flo wanted to know one thing from her mother - who her dad was. She thought this cancer diagnosis would change her mother's mind about telling her his name. Lil had refused to tell Flo who her father was … ever. Flo was still searching for a way to define herself...explain herself. She thought knowing who her father was would help. Lil did not. Lil stood firm. Again, mother and daughter did not speak for two years. Eventually, Flo accepted the fact she would probably never know her dad. It was painful and hurt her deeply, but she didn't want it to become another obstacle mother and daughter must overcome to become, at least, friends.

Flo knew, before her mother's next words, the cancer had returned. Her mom had been diagnosed seven years ago with breast cancer. She had a mastectomy and chemotherapy.

The mastectomy was bad, but Lil had recovered. The chemo was hell. The nausea was uncontrollable. The alteration of senses, the numbness and tingling of fingers and toes were hard for her to bear. Lil swore she would never go through that again. She held true to her word. Once that cancer returned, Lil refused all treatment.

"The cancer is back. It is in the bone now too. I've decided to enjoy the time I have with my Lil and all my family, honey. I hope you understand my choice." Mom measured her words to her daughter. She was still unsure of her forming relationship with the baby girl, now a woman, when she had so heartlessly abandoned her all those years ago. Lil looked at that long ago time like it was a dream. It seemed to have happened to someone else, not her. She knew she should never have become a mother at all. She knew she was not good at it. But here she was, many years later, forming a friendship with her firstborn child. Part of the reason for this was the fact that Lil felt safe enough to come out of the closet and admit she was a lesbian. This was her secret torment for years. She could not say who she really was and she blamed the world... she blamed her child.

Lil had had children with different men, but it was because marriage and childbearing was what was expected of women. When she understood that this was not in her heart, she finally told the family and made many apologies for past behaviors.

The struggle inside her came out in her anger against the world, and against the child that had reminded her, of the lack of acceptance for those like her. She knew the apologies did not make up for everything.

Now, she was thinking about her eldest child. She knew her daughter would be able to handle her eventual death. Flo had lost a child and a husband. A mother who was never really a mother seemed so insignificant after that. Still, Lil thought, I should call someone near her to be sure she is all right. Lil called Joseph.

Joseph was Flo's latest ex-husband. They had remained friends after the arrest. Yes, arrest. Joseph was a bigamist. Six months after their marriage, Flo found out he had never legally divorced his first wife. She called the police and had him arrested. He understood her anger. He was truly sorry. Eventually they had become friends. Lil had liked Joseph too. He still lived near Flo and Lil did call him that day.

"Hey Flo. Your mom just called and told me the news. Are you okay? Can I do anything?" Joseph was truly concerned about both Flo and Lil. It showed in his voice. "I'm fine Joseph. It was shocking after all this time, but we all knew it would come back eventually. Cancer is like that, isn't it?" Flo liked talking to Joseph. He cared about her mom. "I have a date tonight, but I can postpone it. Let me take you for a drink and we can talk about it some more," Joseph suggested. "No, I'm fine. Go on your date and have fun."

Flo hung up the phone and went to the stove to make a cup of tea. It was her wonder drug. She was raised to believe it helped everything. As she was curling up to sip the hot liquid, she thought of her mom. Flo realized she would miss her; maybe the concept of her more than the actual woman. She had longed for her mother for so long. She cried herself to sleep many nights. She wondered why other children had loving mothers and she didn't. She loved to spend time in friends' homes when she was growing up. She would do anything to help in the homes, if it involved helping the mothers. She longed for a mother's approval. Suddenly, she did want that drink. She picked up the phone and called Joseph.

The bar was called The Homestead. Flo thought it a dive. The drink was good and Joseph, for all his own faults, did understand her. She was glad she did this. The bar was not full. When people came and went, everyone noticed. When the door opened about halfway through their second drink, both looked to see who had come in the door. There were three of them; all wore work boots. One was not the type to be noticed if he were the only person in the room. One was a friendly looking man who obviously knew Joseph. They yelled hello's across the bar. The third was tall, quiet, and cute as hell. Flo couldn't stop staring. Joseph joined the newly arrived group for a game of pool.

"Are you going to stop staring and say hello to him?" Joseph was smiling in a teasing sort of way. Flo looked at him, straight-faced, and said, "Joseph, you know how I was raised. I do not talk to men I do not know, especially in a bar. I haven't even been properly introduced." Joseph retorted with a "Well la di da da." They continued their game and Joseph, being the least experienced with a pool cue, left the game early and began to play the poker machine in the far end of the bar. Joseph kept an eye on Flo who kept an eye on the tall, cute man in work boots.

Joseph came back to Flo after a few minutes to check on her drink and get some change for the machine. He stopped to chat with the group, still caught up in playing pool, on his way. "Look, they are going to leave after this game. I'll be finished sooner than that. If you don't talk to him by the time I'm done, I'm going to tell him I'm your ex. Then, I'm going to tell him I have a date and I'm late. I'll ask him if he can take you home as a favor to me. You know how guys are. We always help each other out." Flo knew Joseph well too. She knew he would do just what he said. She could feel the panic inside her begin to rise. Now what? She knew she had a few short minutes. Joseph went back to his machine and he lost that game quickly. The sound of pool cues, thrown on felt covered slate, alerted Flo that she was out of time. Joseph had lost his game and was walking towards the group. Shit! Time's up.

The tall cute one had put on his coat and was walking toward the door behind Flo. Joseph altered his course. Flo willed herself to move. She reached out and grabbed the cute one's arm at elbow level. He stopped cold. Their eyes met. Flo knew she had to find words. "Are you leaving?" Oh, how stupid those words had sounded, even to her. The cute one looked down his arm – slowly – to where her hand still had a firm hold. He looked at his coat. He moved his head, slower than before, to the door behind them. "Uh, yeah," he said. "Why?" Quick. Think. "If you leave, I won't have anyone to talk to except my ex-husband," Flo said, hoping she didn't sound too coy. He stared at her and said, "Ex-husband?" Then he took her hand off his arm and placed it gently on the bar. His coat was off as he sat on a barstool beside her and said, "My name is Brian. Brian Hunt."

Yes. I married him. Three days after meeting in the bar, he moved in with me. Nine months later, we were married. We are still married. My mother died before the wedding. Sometimes, in our grief and pain, we can find happiness. Her death was more difficult than I expected. I still cry out for her like I did as a child, whenever I am in pain. Once, during a surgical procedure, I cried so loudly that the nurse said, "Tell me where she is. I'll get her." "That'll be a trick," I said. "She's dead." Mom was never there for the little pains that happen when a child grows up, but strangely, she is always there for me in death.

There were many husbands, many men, after Len. I married him right out of high school. When he died, whether solely from grief or from the illness I will find I have later, I lived out the years I missed; those years that should have been spent in college or in Europe finding myself.

I am not proud of some of the things I did during that wild time. But, I do not regret that I did them. Each one shaped who I am now. If a piece were to be removed, I would not be the same. Some things did have, and continue to have, repercussions. I am learning how to deal with them.

I face the consequences of my actions and I now teach that actions do hold an inherent responsibility inside them. Nothing in life exists in a vacuum. One of the best lessons I have learned is to be responsible for my actions.

This ends the years before the crash. Each action and event thus far, have set my life's views and built my ability to survive hardships. A reader may say I am a survivor after reading my story so far. It would be a premature assumption. Sometimes the outside of a house looks good, but the inside isn't structurally sound. Remember, I am waiting for the earthquake. I 'got through' the hardships in my life. I did not survive them. I did not know the difference yet. I do now. To describe the difference is ineffable. Read on...

A Life Altering Event, Part One

Flo was tired of proving herself to men in this 'man's world' in which we live. She was savvy and had many good ideas. First, she had to make them listen, truly listen, to her. Today, she would do just that. Flo was a speaking for her company at a regional meeting. Every important person from the east coast would be there listening to her. All the important, career making people, mostly men, would be listening to her ideas and her plans and her thoughts for the future of the business. She had not been in this company as long as the other speakers. She was acutely aware that her future in the company depended on her performance. Every word she would speak that night was written down and rehearsed to perfection. Every nuance was well practiced. Nothing left to chance. She was in control. Ah! Tonight, she would learn that everything cannot be planned; chance is much more powerful than all the planning and control that she could have mustered in her lifetime.

Flo checked her eyes as she left the house that particular morning. A tear formed on the outer corner of one perfectly made up eye. A quick, but expert, flick of a tissue and it was gone. Soon, she was in her car grabbing her sunglasses, hiding any trace of the tear that had been there, but not the memory of it. Flo would remember that tear later.

The clothes fit her to perfection. The long black skirt was chosen because it moved in an ethereal way that was more enchanting than sexual. The softly flowing white blouse was chosen because it complemented the darkness of the skirt beautifully. Long sleeved and high necked, the blouse looked virginal. The black and white jacket pulled everything together and gave her the effect she was looking for; Flo was noticeable enough to grab attention with a look her way and professional enough to complement her words that evening, not distract from them. She had one chance to do this right, and she had to make sure everything was perfect.

Flo chose her accessories to complement her clothing. Simple gold wedding band. Black banded watch. Tiny pearl earrings. Single strand pearl necklace. Elegant. Non-distracting. Classic. Though she always favored the bigger the better school of thought, it was not the time for her jewelry to outshine her message tonight. It was time to get out from behind that computer! She wanted that more than anything. She was ambitious enough. More than that – she was ready.

The hotel was splendid. It reminded Flo of a beloved hotel in England. The room where she would be speaking was a magical place with gilt, crystal and flowers everywhere. It was a ballroom where dreams could come true.

Flo remembered the stories of princesses and princes that were read to her as a child. The belief she had in fairy tales, especially when she was with Frankie during those wonderful British summers, was with her tonight. Fairytales could be set in a place such as this. She still believed in fairytales. She still believed in happily ever after. She still believed she was in control.

Flo did not hesitate when it was her turn to speak. She purposefully walked to the podium and began her speech, the speech that would take her from behind a computer to her own office, with confidence and authority. She heard her voice, loudly and clearly, echoing through the ballroom.

She had finally had her moment. She knew they had heard every word and not merely listened politely the way one must at functions such as this. Flo wanted to make an impact, an impression. She had. The sound of the applause, after her concluding remarks, had let her know she had been heard and understood.

Afterward, as people mingled for the cocktail hour, she was approached by many of the regional executives who complimented her powerful words. The feeling of being in control was feeding her soul this evening. Flo was sure this would be a changing point in her life. She was right; it would be a life-changing night.

Her employer commented approvingly. He stated she was professional and convincing with her ideas about improving the company. He requested that she join some of the out of state people, along with some staff from the office and some executives from another branch, for a late night supper at a local restaurant. Flo was flattered and promptly agreed.

Had she not felt herself floating on a cloud after her speech that night, would she have seen what was happening? Flo would ask herself that question over and over for a very long time. Sometimes, at certain moments, she still does. The plans were made to meet in another area; an area was chosen that was unfamiliar to Flo. "Don't worry," she was told. Someone from the company offered to drive her car to the meeting place. He was with an out of town partner, and that person would drive his car. It was a plan that, at least, would get Flo there. She could worry about getting home later. She agreed.

Flo was sitting at the bar area of the restaurant when people from the meeting had begun to trickle in, but not many at all. Surely there would be more arriving soon, she thought. Her employer, a tall figure with an imposing name, arrived and sat beside her. He told her there was a delay in leaving and the others would be arriving shortly. He slipped away to talk to those already there.

As Flo was finishing her glass of wine, her employer returned and offered her another drink. She had had two drinks already and politely declined. Looking around the restaurant, Flo saw the others in her group begin to leave! Strange, she thought. She turned to her employer who quickly saw the concern in her face and, smiling a most charming smile, he told her that the plans had changed and they would be meeting up elsewhere. He pulled her chair out for her and said she could follow him with her car. She did.

The next restaurant was a few minutes away, and much closer to the Northway, so she would be able to get home afterwards. Once again, Flo was sitting at a bar. She had ordered a glass of water with lemon and, watching the condensation forming on the outside of her glass, she waited for her employer, who was outside talking to someone he had met in the lobby, to come in and tell her where the group would be sitting. He came in alone and sat next to her. "Odd," she thought. The others should have been here first. They left before she did. Glancing at her glass, she thought the trickles of moisture, now running down in slow motion rivulets, looked like tears.

Her employer ordered a drink and began discussing the meeting and Flo's presentation. He told her she would have a new destiny after this evening. Gone were the days of being an office clerk. She was moving up at last. She was excited, she had done it! Flo could see her new future coming true, but she did not know the *true* meaning of his words ... yet.

After talking for about half an hour, Flo began to feel uneasy. She wanted to go home. She had not slept well last night. She never slept well before important events. She always expected something to go wrong, something to ruin them. This was a throwback to her childhood, when her mother found a way to ruin most events and holidays important to Flo by planning her tidal wave entrances and traumatic exits. She asked her employer when the others would be arriving. He made a call and told her everyone had gotten too tired and went home or back to their hotel. Flo was angry at this development. She told him that she was leaving too.

At first, her employer was apologetic, but then he asked her to stay and have dinner and a few drinks with him. Flo thought this a bit odd, but thought he was just being polite after the evening did not go as planned. She told him she preferred to go home and get some rest. He nodded in understanding and asked her where she had parked.

When they had arrived, the restaurant was full. Flo had found a parking space, far from both the building and the lights of the main road, in a place next to the adjoining woods. Her employer, she had noticed, parked directly in front of the door to the restaurant. She knew, from that one thing, that he was a regular here. That did not surprise her. He offered to drive her to her car and see that she got in it safely. Once again he pulled out her chair ... then, he pulled her world out from under her.

THE CRASH

Click. Doors locked. Engine roared. Movement. Stop. Sudden.

Keys jingle. Hand emptied. Safety gone. Her keys. Taken.

Stop.

Can't breathe!

Blackness. Pulling. Ripping. Screams. Silence. Beating.

Teeth. Biting. Hands. Thrusting. Fingers. Probing. Pain.

Windows. Shadowed. Headlights. Bright. Faces. Looking. Blind.

Stop!

Can't breathe!

Pleading. Begging. Screaming. Crying. Hurting. Bleeding.

Entering. Heaving. Panting. Thrusting. Sweating. Coming.

Stop!

Can't breathe!

Doors locked. Engine roared. Movement. Stop. "Get out!"

A tear formed on the outer corner of one, once perfectly made up, eye.

A Life Altering Event, Part Two

Later, after the chaos of arriving home and finding the words – any words because there were no 'right' words – to tell her husband what had happened, she found herself in the Emergency Room of the local hospital. Her mind was operating in flashes. She knew she went home. She knew her best friend had come to the house after her husband, not knowing what to do, made a frantic call for her to help him.

Flo didn't remember going to the hospital, just like she couldn't remember driving home. Her mind had stopped working when 'he' threw her out of his car. Flo had run to her car, but she knew he had stopped his car behind hers. He was blocking her escape once more. Fumbling with her keys he had returned to her after he used her body, clothes torn, bruised with his teeth marks on her breasts and inner thighs, pantyhose in tatters hanging from her legs in wisps plastered against her with his wetness and her blood, she watched as he got out of his car and faced her. Her first thought – "He's going to kill me now." Never could she have guessed what he wanted at that moment. "Do you need directions home?" he asked in a normal conversational tone. Flo was astounded. She stopped trying to find the lock on her car.

She looked at him, stunned, and he drove away. With the fading of his tail lights, Flo's mind began to fade too. Now, as she lay on the gurney in the emergency room, her mind shut down completely.

This is the end of the 'Flo' that I was. I think I died that night - the night of the rape. The problem was that I didn't know how to be reborn. I hadn't the necessary life skills.

I had built my life on fear – the fear of abandonment. I had been 'good,' I had been 'bad,' and I had tried to be so many things in-between. I had tried to be whatever I thought was expected of me, by each person in my life. As a result, I was no one. I had not formed an identity. I was a chameleon. I knew how to adapt. The only problem with that was that it was never the 'real' me, so it was never permanent.

I had my false sense of security until that night – control. I had danced through my life in a strange waltz with reality. I had picked up the pieces and begun again so many times that I believed nothing could touch me. I mean really touch me.

People said I was cold, heartless, and had no feelings. Was it history repeating itself? Did I hear those words said about my mother? It never bothered me. I couldn't see the need for something with so much potential to destroy you. It had worked for me up until that night

... the night I crashed in my tunnel

... the night I died.

Coming Out of the Tunnel

Chapter One - **Beginning**

Help me! The echoes of that night wash over me like a tide.
Reality is now the dream, the way of life for me.
Sanity...is the only hope.
Sleep...no longer a reprieve.
Death...is my only escape.
Help me! The echoes of that night wash over me...
And I am drowning.
F. D. Hunt

Flo didn't remember the first time she tried to kill herself. She didn't like to use the word suicide.10 It is too neat, too clean, and too sterile for what is really happening. It is the killing of the self. "Maybe," Flo thought, "I would go as far as saying it was a mercy killing... but killing is what it is. Maybe it is murder: A murder of the tormented soul."

Flo's husband, Brian, was the first to know that something was wrong. Flo came to bed. That alone was a clue. She did not sleep in their bed any longer. She didn't feel safe, not even there. Flo slept, with all the lights on, in her recliner in the living room. It was the way she said goodnight that gave Brian pause. There was finality in her voice and it had unnerved him. He said it made him afraid. He's glad that it did. He saved Flo that night.

Flo woke up...no... she faded up into consciousness in a cloudy dream. She tasted being awake before she felt it. The charcoal, which was used to pump her stomach, felt gritty and tasted like freshly dug dirt in her mouth. It felt as if she had been buried alive and had clawed her way up from the dark, heaving and gasping mouthfuls of loamy earth along the way. Hazy darkness loomed around her as she struggled to keep some distant flashes of light in her focus. Slowly, and after much strain on her part, Flo could make out hazy shapes surrounding her. The shapes seemed to move lazily and dreamily back and forth in a silent rhythmic dance. All at once, like the flick of a light switch, Flo saw the shapes were people.

When she could make out the faces, Flo realized that her family was standing over her and that she was in a bed. They were speaking, but no sounds reached her ears. Gaping mouths opening and closing made her begin to shake with an unexpected fear. A tinkling sound, bell like in quality, made it through and she registered it. Someone had rung for a nurse thinking she was convulsing. A needle appeared and after a brief sting, she slept again... peacefully.

Earlier that evening, Flo sat calmly in front of the TV set. Her husband had gone to bed less than an hour ago. Though the television was on, Flo did not see whatever program playing. She was lost in the thoughts of her life since the brutal assault.... or rather her lack of life. It all seemed so pointless now.

The motions of day to day survival were enormous challenges that she had to force herself to overcome. She was now at the point where most of them had gotten the best of her. Flo no longer dressed. Pajamas were all she could manage. She rarely washed. She had not worn make up since that fateful night that seemed a lifetime ago.

Now, staring blankly into the show of her life playing on the screen in her mind, she wished to stop the endless reruns. The bottle of sleeping pills, on the table beside her, lay on its side. The small neon orange and bright white capsules were strewn across the tabletop like an unstrung necklace of psychedelic pearls. One by one, Flo picked up the colored jewels and swallowed them with a sip of her tea.

The suicide attempts and hospital stays kept happening. Flo kept wishing that people would just let her die. They did not. Fate intervened time after time for two and a half years. There was always an intervention at the critical moment. She wished nothing but to die and see her daughter Amy once again.

Suicide attempts sometimes have triggers. Flo's trigger was her loss of control, her realization that she had trusted and was betrayed. This was a common occurrence during the time of investigation and trial preparation. She learned that victims are sometimes treated worse than criminals.

Though the district attorney had been sympathetic and understanding and believed her, the grand jury lacked enough evidence for a conviction. They had to choose not to have her rapist indicted. The hospital had botched the rape kit; the young PA on duty had let her torn and tattered clothes be thrown away. All evidence was gone but for the memories in Flo's mind.

The police were less than sympathetic. Flo had chosen not to report the rape until she had seen her family doctor and a therapist. The rape crisis counselor had told her this was a good choice. It was. She was hospitalized the first time after speaking to the police in the safety of her therapist's office. She was fragile then. It would have been much worse if Flo had tried to report the rape without any support. This decision, however, skewed the police view of her as a victim. After all, wouldn't she have reported this right away if it were true?

After Flo had left the mental health unit of the hospital that first time she had tried to end her life, the police picked her up within minutes of her discharge and asked her to come with them. They wanted her to identify two different restaurants that were common hangouts for her attacker.

Flo, unfamiliar as she was with the area where she had been, did not remember the name or address of the places she had visited that night.

The police told her it was their job to figure that out. Of course, she went with them willingly. She trusted them. They were police officers – but they were worse than her rapist - evil in the guise of good.

When a still medicated Flo exited the police car at the first building, the officers asked her if this was the place where the rape had happened. Flo, wanting to be right, wanting to remember, wanting to please, walked around the front of the building. She wasn't sure.

She needed to see inside. They told her they could not get in yet. It was early in the morning. But, they would take her to the other place they suspected, and return here if necessary. Again, Flo got in the squad car with the safe State Police logo on the doors, and once again she stepped into a nightmare.

A walk around this second building began a shaking in Flo's soul. The owner lived next door so this building could be entered. One officer stayed with Flo while the other went to roust the owner from, almost assuredly, a needed slumber. In a robe the color of the house red, the owner emerged from the comfort of his home. He pulled the worn robe tightly around him as if he felt Flo's shivers, shuffled across the lot, and opened the front door.

Flo walked in first, being propelled forward by the forceful hands of both police officers, but she never made it past the lobby. This was the place!

Waves of nausea engulfed her and rolled over her body in the same way flames would roll in the vacuum of space. The soft bright undulating rolls carried certain pain. Flo saw flashes of what took place that evening a few weeks ago. It seemed like it was happening to her now – again.11 Knees that were barely holding her weight now went weak and she slid to the floor against the wall. Sobs wracked her body.

The owner of the restaurant went to reach for her. Pity flooded his eyes. It was as if he saw his daughter or sister or wife in Flo. A police officer stopped him by grabbing his arm roughly. "Let her alone, the lying drunken bitch." The other officer mumbled something in agreement. Both officers began yelling at her. "Why didn't you know the other place wasn't the place right away?" "You are such a drunken liar." "You are coming to the barracks with us right now." "We need your statement before you can make up any more lies."

Once at the barracks, Flo was subjected to the stereotypical good cop, bad cop routine and kept in a small, windowless room for eight hours. Treated as suspect, not a victim, she was unable to leave, not allowed a drink or to go to the toilet, and when tracked down by her rape crisis counselor, Flo was not allowed to see her. She suffered horrors worse than the rape itself... a broken trust. These were trusted public servants. The betrayal was almost deadly. Flo's life spark, her essence, humanity, or any other euphemism one may use to represent the 'soul' of a human being, went out.

Those first days after the rape were still a blur to Flo. She had gone to the hospital, reported the assault to the police, had a rape crisis counselor, saw her own doctor, went to a psychologist, but still, less than a week later, Flo was in the hospital after suffering an emotional collapse. Because the police had treated her so viciously when she was released, Flo took the advice of her counselor and hired a lawyer.

Rick was sweet and soft spoken. He had not been a lawyer for very long, but he knew the odds of prosecuting the attacker were slim. He also knew the man should be held responsible somehow. He suggested waiting to see if there would be an indictment, and then proceeding with a civil suit to cover medical expenses. Flo and her husband agreed. Rick also instituted a complaint against the police officers involved. Though assured an internal affairs investigation would be conducted, Rick told Flo she would never know the outcome. Police are a protected species.

Rick, the young but wise lawyer, suggested that Flo begin a journal in the early days after the rape.12 The writing would be a way of remembering what was difficult to think about. It became a map of Flo's journey in those early days. While most of it was facts and events Flo could remember so there would be documentation for court, some of those writings were the raw feelings and ravings of a tortured soul...

"Why did he do this to me?... I don't understand life...

What a sword to have over your head – not knowing when you will relive the most horrible experience in your life again, and again, and again... I feel like I will never recover from any of this – it will haunt me forever... I am filled with fears and there is room for nothing else...

I am afraid everywhere...

I don't think I'll ever feel safe again... My rape crisis counselor told me about the night in the emergency room. She said I was fragile. Funny word... fragile. I guess people can shatter like delicate porcelain too. I know I did. I cried when she was telling me. It was like she was talking about someone else, but I knew she meant me... I am tired. I want all this to stop. Can anyone really help me, please help me...

I hurt so much. I just keep hurting.

What did I do to deserve this?

How do I make this pain stop? I live in fear and pain. I think it is better just to die... I am dying inside – slowly and painfully. I don't know what to do.

Can anyone ever help me...

I feel like a burden on family and friends. I don't think they know how to treat me. I can't blame them. I don't know how to treat me either... I feel worthless, useless, a burden to everyone.

Why can't I just die?

   ... I can't do this anymore. I am done...

The first two and a half years after the rape was lost time for me; I felt betrayed by life itself. I have few memories of this dark time and I think that is probably one of life's small blessings.

Getting through the civil trial was exceptionally brutal. While laws are in place to protect criminal rape victims, there are no laws protecting these victims in a civil trial.13 My life's history was free game for the many attorneys on my rapist's defense team. I had a single, local young attorney. My attacker had a team from Albany, New York City, and Washington, DC.

There were three days of depositions for me, while my assailant had one – barely. During this time I suffered migraines and the medication I took, a narcotic, seemed to give me strength. It was not long before I took those pills for more than physical pain. It is easy to reach for comfort in any form. I self-medicated myself into oblivion. I was lucky. I survived. But it took another death to bring me back to life once more.

CHAPTER 2 - **Changing**

Flo was lost. She had ceased all therapy her family doctor had initiated for her. She became more and more agoraphobic. Shut off from the world outside her home, she would not talk to anyone - even on the telephone. She was shut down. She was suspended in time. She had ceased to exist. Though she was as sure as she could be that she was no longer suicidal, she was not sure of anything else. Where was her control? Where was her life going? What was she supposed to do? Flo could no longer be the person she was before the rape. She didn't know if she wanted to be 'her' anymore. To be honest, she still didn't know if she really wanted to live.

Then, fate interceded in Flo's life once more. It was quite early in the morning on the 31st of August 1997. Tower Bridge was looming, large and splendid, on the television screen in her living room. The Thames, with its muddy London blue topaz waters slowly drifting underneath, glowed softly under the beautifully lit bridge. Flo thought of London and her life long ago. Her life's blood was the Thames. It ran through her veins once ... long, long ago.

Flo watched the end of her favorite video. She saw a last glimpse of her favorite city, her favorite home, and then the slow roll of credits began to swim endlessly over the screen.

Three things happened quite simultaneously. There was the sound of the soft mechanical click of the VCR shifting into rewind mode, the cable TV channel began to come into focus, and there was a loud and startling ring of the telephone. Flo grabbed the phone and heard her son yelling, "Mom! Mom! Turn on the TV! Princess Diana died!" before the receiver reached her ear. Shocked, she mumbled something of acknowledgment to him, promised she would turn on the news, and hung up the phone. Turning her head slowly, she looked at the television and watched her world changing again.

"Diana, Princess of Wales, is dead." Flo would always remember the hollowness of the news announcer's words; words she would never forget. Her world went dark as her vision narrowed and she dropped to the floor in the black haze of a panic attack. The swift pounding of her heart sent blood rushing through her body. She could hear her heartbeat echoing in her head. She thought, for a brief moment, she must have heard wrong. But, the words Flo had just heard began scrolling across the bottom of the screen. As she reached out a hand to touch those words, to feel if they were real, she felt the soft, slick wetness of tears on her cheeks. She remembered a tear she had carelessly flicked from her eye long ago, before her world changed – before she crashed in her tunnel.

This world, her new world, that she was struggling so hard to make some sense of for more than two years, was suddenly ripped apart ...again.

The tragedies of her life played in her head. The death of her own princess, Amy ... her husband's death in a motorcycle accident ... her mother's death from breast cancer... and the many more deaths of those she loved, including her beloved great granny, Emily. Then, Flo thought of her own 'death,' the rape – her own crash in the tunnel... of her own life.

She had spent over two years in the darkness of her tunnel. Her life was a dark blur. Consumed in this haze of twilight existence, she could not find her way back. She could not see the light. She could not feel safe. She felt raw, bruised, rotted. Life hurt. Videos and television shows about her beloved England was the only thing that seemed to make her existence bearable. Curled like a baby in her favorite chair, Flo would watch them for hours. They were her refuge. Now – this!

"Diana, Princess of Wales, is dead." Flo could feel the darkness around her and inside her. Once again, life had shown her that safety is an illusion. We, none of us, are ever really safe ... are we? The rug beneath her face was damp as she slowly pushed herself up. She didn't remember falling down. She looked up at the television and, for the first time, saw the car that had held the life of the Princess of Wales in its steel and glass womb. Flo wondered if Diana knew, in the moments before that awful impact, her fate...her destiny. She wondered if Diana had felt any pain. It must have happened so fast. Flo knew that many would feel grief and sadness for Diana, and her sons, during the weeks to follow.

Watching the events unfold during the week until Princess Diana's funeral, Flo grieved as if Diana had been a beloved friend or family member. Flo had watched with the world as this woman, who grew from a rosebud into an English rose, came into full bloom. Now, she would be an eternal rose. Diana was a woman with an abundance of compassion that transcended time and distance and touched you - personally. You did not have to know her to be touched by the special kind of love she projected: Empathetic Love.

The art of commiseration was easy with her. When she spoke of feeling as though she were raped when hounded and photographed unabashedly by paparazzi, Flo had understood. She empathized with Diana too. Flo knew, therefore, that Diana would understand her pain and, in turn, empathize with her. Princess Diana was a friend to many people she never knew, never met, just because they too, felt she would understand their pain. She was also as flawed as they were. She knew this, and admitted it openly. This made her the epitome of hope. It was her gift. She gave her gift freely, without expectation, but always with love.

It's hard to move forward after a profound event – a life altering event. Life does go on. How you choose to live it is a tribute. It is a tribute to those who are gone and to those yet to come. It is a tribute to those who have overcome tragic events and those who could not. But, most of all, how you live your life is a tribute to yourself.

Flo saw the meaning in these words now. For the first time in two and a half years, Flo was beginning to understand what needed to happen next. Flo needed to live!

It's funny how someone else's tragedy can often inspire us. Flo thought about how we often become so enveloped in our own 'crashes' that it takes the crash of another to jolt our bruised psyches. We retain empathy for others, but not for ourselves. Maybe this occurs on purpose. It is often easier to think clearly from a distance. It gives us perspective. It allows us time to move on.

It wasn't easy for Flo to make the decisions she now had to make. First, she had to find another therapist. She needed a guide on this journey. Now, for the first time since that night, Flo wanted to make the changes she needed to give her life meaning. She felt her first glimmers of hope. She wanted to live. She wanted to rebuild her life. She wanted to come back to the world she thought had abandoned her. She realized she had abandoned it. It was always there. It was waiting for her now.

Life was calling her once again. This time, Flo heard.

It was difficult for me to realize I needed to return to therapy. I had slipped back so far. I knew I had so much hard work ahead of me. I still work hard. I have had other serious setbacks since my return to therapy. I call it my return to the living.

Life will probably always be a struggle for me, but at this time, I realized I was forming a plan. I was beginning, ever so slowly, to regain my control. Not the fictional control I had believed I had since I was a toddler, but a real control...one where I would know that there are always going to be some things that would be out of my control. I would have to find a way to live with that knowledge.

Therapy would be the only hope of doing what I now realized I would do...live! I would go on. I would be a different person from the one I was before the crash, my crash, but that was all right. I knew I had much work to do. I would find a way to redefine myself. I wanted to show how adversity could be overcome. I wanted to inspire. I wanted to be able to reach out and transcend time and space...and touch someone too.

Walls

Walls surround me in my self-made prison.
Not so much keeping me in, but keeping the world out.
I talk...through walls.
I see...through walls.
I touch...through walls.
Someday, these walls will crack.
Part of me will spill out.
Then... the walls will crumble.
I will be able,
To talk ...
To see ...
To touch ...

By F. D. Hunt

Chapter Three - **Returning**

The road back to life had begun. Flo knew the road would still have many obstacles and detours, but she was ready this time. Therapy, begun a few days after the attack, was never productive. Often, Flo left her psychologist's office feeling more empty and withdrawn than when she entered. The therapist herself did not seem to want to help Flo out of the blackness in which she had found herself enveloped. Eventually, Flo just stopped going.

Flo thought she was a strong person. A strong person would need no help other than herself. Hadn't she survived until now? Hadn't she suffered great losses? Naively, Flo thought she could survive anything, but it was not so. She had not. But now, now at this moment, Flo was sure she would survive. She understood the need for a guide out of the forest of darkness she had been lost in for so long. It was different this time. Flo felt it. She knew it. She would make it happen this time. Flo began her return to life.

The second 'first day' of therapy was quite different indeed. Flo had chosen to go to the outpatient behavioral health unit of the hospital she had spent so much time in since the night her world had collapsed. If the inpatient unit had been able to keep her alive until now, she was sure the psychologists and doctors of the outpatient unit could give her the will to stay alive and get her life back.

Donna, her new therapist, was a petite and quiet woman. She sat patiently that first day, waiting for Flo to talk. Flo sat, just as quietly, and wondered for a moment, if she had made a mistake to try this again. What if she could never come back from this feeling of powerlessness that was consuming her soul? Feeling very tiny and afraid, Flo stared at the floor and disappeared into her darkness.

Suddenly, a quiet and calm voice reached into the blackness surrounding Flo. The voice carried with it a soft muted light that penetrated through the darkness like a beacon. "Flo, it was a beautiful day today when you had to come here. I bet the sun felt good. I love that warm feeling when the sunlight shines on your skin and you feel like you are glowing. Do you like the sun too? - Maybe you prefer the rain. Some people love the sound of the rain. It is soothing to the mind. The grey clouds and soft mist can sometimes make one feel anonymous and some like that much better than the light." Donna sat and waited once again.

Slowly, Flo raised her head and looked at Donna. She thought about the question. She tried to read Donna. She tried to access what answer Donna was looking for with her question. She wanted to be good. She wanted to give the 'right' answer. Donna did look safe to Flo, but Flo did not trust her judgment anymore.

Flo didn't feel like getting up and running, physically or mentally, the way she had every time she set foot in the other therapist's office. She decided to answer the question honestly, with her own genuine feelings.

"I like the sun. I like being warm. I prefer the rain. I like to feel the sense of aloneness that rain allows. When it's sunny, everyone feels they can approach you, talk to you; but, when it's raining, people are just interested in getting to where they are going to get inside and be dry. No one has time for talking. People walk by each other looking at the ground for puddles or at the sky to see if is going to stop raining. Everything seems muted and the sound of the rain is always there like white noise. Sun is nice. Rain is better."

Flo looked at Donna and tried to judge her reaction to the answer she had just given. Donna was clearly thinking. Flo could see it in her face. It was a face that didn't try to hide anything at all. She seemed to be trying to form a thought and Flo knew she would speak shortly.

"When people talk to you does it hurt like when the sun is bright and shining in your eyes?"

Flo was taken aback by the way Donna had actually listened to her and understood the feelings behind her words. "Yes. It hurts. I just want to close my eyes and never open them again."

Well, let's see if we can bring you back into the sun."

Therapy had begun.

> *It wasn't easy – those first months of therapy. I had assumed that I would be talking about the assault itself. I had assumed we would explore what it had done to my soul, my psyche, and my control. I learned that to reclaim myself, I had to first figure out who I was. I had to revisit my past.*

> *In my sessions with Donna, I began the slow and painful journey of examining the little girl left in the crib because she was of no value. But, even before that journey began, I needed to find a way to exist in a world that had become frightening to me. Donna gave me tools, tricks, skills, to begin to venture out into this frightening world. I began to move from the safety of my recliner to 'outside,' once again.*

Donna taught me to breathe through my fear. It was difficult to have anyone behind me. Supermarkets were akin to a Halloween haunted house. In those early days, I would often leave the grocery cart and run.

Using breathing techniques, I began to work through this small and taken for granted, everyday activity. I would hear Donna in my head saying, "Hold the cart, use the feel of the handle to ground yourself, and walk slowly," Session after session, I became stronger and stronger. I began to reenter the world. I crawled into the world at first. I soon began to walk.

Now, I run.

Chapter Four - **Dogs.**

Flo had never known a time in her life that had not included a dog. When she was very young, and living in England, there was Brandy. Brandy was a Cocker Spaniel the color of fine cognac hit by golden rays of sunshine. She literally glowed. She was a warm and inviting gold. Brandy was the pride and joy of Flo's Aunt Margaret and Uncle Gordon. Four times a day, without fail, Flo would hear her aunt's voice echo through the house. "Brandy! Walkies!" It was Aunt Margaret's only real form of exercise, unless one was to count the morning stretches Aunt Margaret did without fail.

Over the years, Flo came to realize that Aunt Margaret always had Brandy. Though a dog's lifespan was not that long, there was a Brandy by her aunt's side for years. Margaret had so loved the first little dog, that when the original had died, another female of the same golden color was promptly purchased. There was always a Brandy until sweet Aunt Margaret could no longer have her 'walkies.'

Flo's first dog of her own was also a Cocker Spaniel. Princess was the color of rich dark cocoa. She was actually shared between Flo and her sister, Debbie. Princess was fierce and full of pearly white and razor sharp puppy teeth.

Flo had experience with puppy teeth. This consisted of the fact that it was better not to experience them! She had learned this with many Brandy's. Debbie had not learned this lesson. One day puppy teeth met painfully and firmly with Debbie's thumb in a very unfriendly manner. Princess became Flo's dog. The ownership, however, was brief.

Princess liked to bite everything ... anything! One evening she tangled with a wild animal in the backyard behind the house. Princess was badly hurt. The vet said she would have a long recuperation and would be blind in one eye and have poor sight in the other. Flo's family talked with the vet and it was decided to find Princess a good home in the country. City life with many cars and busy streets would not be good for the very ill puppy. Flo and Debbie said their sad and tearful good-byes, and Princess went to live on a farm owned by the vet.

Shortly after this, Flo's family was rocked by the sad news that Flo's Uncle Billy, the very one who named her, had cancer. It was almost Easter and it would be a sad holiday. It reaffirmed Flo's hatred of holiday times.

Shortly after his diagnosis, Uncle Billy came to the house one day and asked to see Flo. He told her he was taking her out for a ride. They drove to the animal shelter where he told Flo to pick out a puppy of her own! Flo was so excited she hugged and kissed her youngest uncle and ran off through the many kennels.

She stopped and looked in every kennel door. She wasn't happy though. Flo wanted to take every one of these sad-eyed pups home with her. The dogs were looking at her and begging for a home. She finally spotted a tiny brown and white ball of fur and pulled on Uncle Billy's hand. "I want that one," she said. "Then you shall have her," said Uncle Billy. "What will you name her?" he asked. Flo thought the little puppy looked like a bunny when she first saw her, and it was almost Easter, so she named her new dog Bunny.

A few short months later, at the young age of twenty nine, Uncle Billy was gone. He left behind a young wife and two small children. He also left behind a wonderful memory he had made with his niece. Flo never forgot that day. She never would.

Eventually, Bunny succumbed to cancer as well. She had lived a long and happy life and had learned many things about her humans. She danced for candy canes at Christmas and for carrots at any time! She loved Flo, but she loved Flo's grandmother best. It was Lillian who took Bunny to the vet the day she died. Lillian cried that day, not just for Bunny, but for the memory of her son that the dog had held for her.

When Flo was older, an adult herself, she still had dogs. Her children had a dog called Rebel. He was a big, clumsy, oafish Irish Setter. He loved the children. They were not too gentle with him and he was not too gentle with them.

Many times there was a tumble of dog and children all tangled together rolling on the floor with giggles and soft dog sounds surrounding them. This big gentle giant was only two and a half when Flo's daughter Amy died. Three days later Rebel died. The vet said he had a broken heart.

During the time Flo was mourning for her daughter, someone gave her a tiny Yorkshire terrier puppy. Flo named her Fruffles, after a cartoon squirrel. Fruffles was Flo's baby and they became inseparable. When Flo decided to mate her dog, she bought a little male Yorkshire terrier and named him Baffi. Loosely translated in Italian, it means whiskers. The puppies were beautiful, and Flo proudly gave them to family and friends. When it came time for both dogs to be spayed and neutered, Flo gave the last puppy of the last litter to her new husband's mother, Margie. She was named Terry and became the daughter Flo's mother in law never had. When Terry died, it broke Margie's heart and she would never own another dog.

Fruffles and Baffi lived long and happy lives. New puppies came into Flo's life, and one day a young one collided with an old and frail Baffi. The vet had to put Baffi down. It was Flo's husband's birthday. A few months later, on Flo's birthday, Fruffles had a stroke. She was taken to the vet in Flo's arms. Flo kept telling the still and tiny dog that she would be all right. Talking to her softly and lovingly as she had to Amy years before, Flo knew Fruffles would die.

Like her grandmother years earlier, Flo would also have a memory of her child at the dog's death. When Amy had died, Flo hadn't been able to hold her daughter since the ride to the hospital when Amy was enveloped in Flo's arms. The tubes, wires, IV's, and other medical equipment made it impossible to do anything other than find a place on Amy's arm to feel her soft skin. When Flo had gone into the hospital room after Amy's death, the wires and tubes were still in place. The only contact between them was a kiss, a brief brush of that wayward blonde curl, and a final feel of her daughter's small hand in hers. Now, holding Fruffles as the vet administered that final injection, Flo felt as though she was holding her daughter at last. Through tears she told the vet and vet tech the story.

Because Flo had gotten Fruffles during her mourning for her much loved daughter, the dog and child were one in Flo's mind. Now she was able to hold her child through her dog's tiny body as she, in her mind, gave Fruffles to Amy. Flo found closure.14 The vet and tech were crying with Flo as she, once again, said her "Last Goodbye."

There have been other dogs, but these, except for one, are the ones that hold the most profound memories.

I have three Yorkies now: Bea, Bitsy, and Boo. They have yet to create their memories.

The 'one' is Moose. His chapter comes next. I loved all of my dogs. I still cannot imagine life without the unconditional love that these wonderful furry creatures give to my soul.

I have used my dogs as perfect listeners, loving partners, and true friends.

They have used me for biscuits.

Chapter Five - **The Dog's Discovery.**

Moose was a male Jack Russell terrier. He was a pup when Fruffles died, but soon he found his own place in Flo's heart. Moose was headstrong, obsessive, and happy only when in Flo's lap or cuddling next to her in bed. He loved to dig and was so high-strung that a feather hitting the ground could send him into a frenzy of barking and jumping until he was sure there was no danger to his humans, and one human in particular. But, with Flo, Moose was calm and docile and never jumped on her or stepped too hard on her lap. He was careful.

One afternoon Flo came home tired. She sat in her recliner to rest before beginning dinner. Moose jumped onto her lap and she pulled a blanket from the top of the chair to make a bed for him. Moose would not lie down. He began to paw frantically at Flo's chest. It was the same movements he made while digging in the garden. It hurt. Flo was shocked. She pushed her dog away and said the words she had never said to him before, "Bad dog!" Moose was unfazed, and he jumped up and did it again. Flo was astounded. She placed Moose on the floor and once again, as soon as his paws hit the floor, he sprung back up into her lap and began 'digging' once again.

Flo got up and walked to the kitchen and began dinner. She thought Moose would forget about it, but as soon as Flo sat down again, Moose was right there pawing on her like he was digging in his favorite spot in the yard. Flo was worried. She wondered if there was something wrong with Moose, but soon she was thinking "What if it is me?" Flo recently saw a documentary where dogs had been trained to smell diseases.15 Something in her, some sense of foreboding, told her she needed to take Moose's strange behavior seriously.

The next morning, Flo called Dr. Serlin, her gynecologist and told him the story. To Flo's amazement, her doctor listened to her. "I know I just had my check-up and mammogram last month and they were fine," she heard herself saying, "but I think there may be something there." Flo knew her family's history with breast cancer. Most of the women in her family had died from it, or it had, in some manner, contributed to their deaths. She felt better when her doctor told her to come see him later that day. The doctor had felt nothing on the exam, and had done another mammogram that was also normal. He sent Flo for one more test, an ultrasound.

That was how the doctor found the lump that the dog discovered.

Within three days Flo had seen a surgeon and was in the hospital having surgery. She was scared. She had seen her mother and aunt die of this horrible disease. She knew what it did. She knew the 'cure' was often as bad as the disease itself. The wait for the pathology results seemed to take forever. The surgeon had to remove more breast tissue than he expected. Flo didn't mind the hollow she would now have in her left breast. She had seen her mother lose both breasts and her aunt lose one. She had seen the effects of both chemotherapy and radiation. She crossed her fingers and prayed. She also cried.

The results came back. ADH. Atypical Ductal Hyperplasia.16 At the time Flo was diagnosed it was considered by some doctors and surgeons to be Stage 0 or Stage 1 breast cancer. Flo was immediately scheduled to see an oncologist. Devastated, Flo wondered what she should do now. The wait to see the next doctor seemed painfully long. Flo was finishing her college courses. It was difficult to concentrate on the coursework. It was difficult to concentrate at all.

The oncologist reassured Flo that though still considered a cancer by some, most considered it a precancerous growth. It was treated in much the same way as an early non-invasive breast cancer would be treated. With Flo's family history, he recommended a double mastectomy with reconstructive surgery. This was a ticking time bomb Flo had in her chest.

Flo was shocked and wondered if this major surgery was the only option open to her. She didn't care about the loss of the breasts; the doctors would be able to do the reconstructive surgery at the same time. Flo worried about the major time frame of recovery this surgery would require. Months of healing. Months of therapy. Flo was concerned with time because she had just lost so much of it.

After a discussion with her husband and much serious thought and researching on her part, Flo returned to the doctor and told him no. She would not do surgery, but she would consider some of the new oral chemotherapy trials she had read about. There was one in her area and she was referred to that study to see if she qualified. She did. A few weeks later, she began the trial and hoped for the best.

The drug she was taking made her quite ill. She felt like she was stuffed into her own skin. Her body swelled and itched and she ached all over. The doctors conducting the study gave her medications to counteract the effects, but eventually, after living through this for a year and a half, Flo left the study.

She met with her doctors again, and they all came to a decision together. They would do what is called 'watchful waiting' with Flo. She would be seen by a doctor every three months and tested more frequently and thoroughly than before the ADH was found. Flo could live with this decision. If cancer was found early, it could then be treated as aggressively as needed.

I have lived this watchful waiting since that time. Recently, lumps were found in the other breast. I had them removed and tested and it was ADH in the other breast too. I have met with my oncologist. My doctors are worried that along with the ADH there could be ductal carcinoma that cannot be seen yet. I am not yet ready to commit to the time that double mastectomy would require. There are new chemotherapy drugs and preventative medications that I may be able to tolerate. I will handle my choices with careful consideration and I will do what is best for me. I will make choices, not to please anyone, not for control, but for me, truly for my own health and peace of mind. That is a very empowering feeling.

Chapter Six - **More than PTSD**

Flo had continued therapy all through the ordeal of finding a 'time bomb' in her breasts. It kept her sane and she had actually been making good progress. She returned to college and, though it was difficult for her, she persevered. She could see the progress she had made since the beginning of her therapy. There were some difficult times when Flo felt she was on a roller coaster out of control; but, she was moving forward and taking back her life. She realized, however, that her life held either sunshine or storms. There seemed to be no cloudy days, just emotionally charged days of black and white – no grey.

Flo had been on medications almost from the beginning of her therapy, but she still felt like she was climbing the walls of her life. This feeling, though really present in Flo throughout all her life in some way, was becoming more pronounced. Flo began to suffer with terrible bouts of insomnia. This began after her rape but, though she was not suffering flashbacks and panic attacks as much as she did during the two and a half years she had been suicidal, the insomnia was getting worse.

Now, sitting in the waiting room at the hospital's outpatient unit, Flo was waiting to meet with her psychiatrist.

She was a wonderfully soft-spoken woman, much like her therapist, Donna, who talked to Flo like a person, not just a patient. After listening to Flo for about twenty minutes, she asked her some simple questions about her past. She looked at Flo and smiled. "I think there is more than PTSD going on here. Tell me more about your mother's behaviors." She began writing as Flo spoke.

When Flo finished speaking, the doctor jotted a few more notes and looked up from the chart. She turned her chair slightly to face Flo without a desk between them. Then, in a soft and reassuring voice, she told Flo, "You have more than simple Post Traumatic Stress Disorder. I am very surprised that no one has picked this up before now. Though you have been functioning well, for the most part, for your entire life actually, there are signs that should have been easy to spot. You have Bipolar Disorder.[17] The PTSD was masking it this time because it can produce very similar symptoms. If you look at your life before the rape, then you will see that you have had symptoms similar to the PTSD through most of your life, even as a child.[18] We used to think that only adults could be bipolar, but now we know that isn't true. I think your mother was bipolar; there is a genetic component to it, and you are bipolar as well." She paused to let Flo absorb what she had just said.

It seemed to make sense. It wasn't the first time Flo had heard the term. It had been used, in its older form, Manic Depression, to describe her mother by various family members. Flo often felt so full of energy that she thought she could conquer the world. She needed little or no sleep. People who were slow annoyed her. Her world became a blur, but she felt, for the most part, more productive than others.

There were also times that she was so sad she just wanted to crawl into a dark hole and die. She even named this hole: The Black Spot. It was a total absence of anything worth living for, anything good and light. The energetic times weren't all wonderful either. Sometimes she couldn't make people understand her. Words seemed to come out of her mouth so fast that she had to struggle to make herself understood. Thoughts and ideas flooded her mind so fast that it took tremendous effort to focus on one at a time. She took risks during those manic times. Sometimes her actions had made her cringe when she settled back to earth. Yes, this did make sense.

The doctor started her on medications and told her that they may have to be changed to find the one, or combination, that worked best for her. Flo was willing to try to bring some shades of grey into her life. She was ready.

It took a long time to find the right combination of medications that worked for me. I had been unable to take either of the two mainstream drugs for Bipolar Disorder: Lithium and Depakote.

It was trial and error for a long time. Sometimes the medications seemed to work for a while, only to result in a full-blown manic episode or depression so striking that I feared I was suicidal again.

Eventually, the right combination was found and I gained an equilibrium of thought I had never experienced before. I was able to make new breakthroughs in my therapy, and focus on my studies.

I had reached a place of calm. I didn't know it then, but this was a turning point for me. I now had a tangible 'disorder' to explain the way I felt sometimes. I wasn't crazy, far from it. I had lacked critical information to make sense of my life.

Being bipolar is not a bad thing. Robin Williams often uses his disorder to spark his creativity when writing his comedy sketches. Google famous people with Bipolar Disorder, and get ready to be surprised. Winston Churchill. Beethoven. Lord Byron. Cole Porter. Bing Crosby...

Chapter Seven - **Mirko**

Donna called Flo into her office for a regular appointment. The two had built a rapport from months of difficult work. The debilitating panic attacks that crippled Flo for the first few years after the rape, had become less frequent and almost manageable. Donna had worked harder than Flo at first. From their first meeting, the bright therapist had seen the borderline traits in Flo. She knew she would need to go slowly in therapy. Trust first, work second. The approach had worked. Flo was working very hard in her therapy now. She had realized Donna would not abandon her. Now she would have to tell her she would be doing just that.

As soon as Flo sat down on the comfortably worn overstuffed chair, her haven of safety for the past few years, Flo knew something was wrong. Donna looked at her and reached across the expanse of their two chairs and touched Flo's hand. "I waited to tell you this because I know this will be hard for you. I didn't want it to interfere with your therapy so I thought it best to wait. I am leaving Glens Falls. I will not be your therapist any longer."

Flo's world began to spin. No! What would she do now? How could she feel comfortable with anyone else? This was so unfair. She had come so far. She realized Donna was still speaking.

"I have chosen a new therapist for you. He has seen your file and has spoken to me extensively about you. I want you to promise me you will give him a chance. It is in your nature to run from changes in your life. Remember, how we talked about perceived abandonment? I am not abandoning you. Your new therapist, Mirko, will not abandon you either. He will give you new insights that you are ready to handle now. Look at this as part of your therapy. It will be rocky at first, but hang in there and see what happens. Will you promise me you will stay in therapy and give Mirko a try?"

Flo was heartbroken, but she had trusted this woman during a time when it was not easy for her to trust. She knew Donna had patiently waited until this trust had built and was solid before challenging her with real work during her therapy sessions. Flo decided she would trust her now. This was a major step for Flo. She had learned how to truly trust someone. She made the promise.

Meeting Mirko was a surprise. He was a very happy man with an enthusiasm that Flo actually envied. He was easy to talk to and Flo thought she would like him that first day. But, she wasn't sure she would be able to confide in a man the way she had with a woman.

She had kept most of what had happened during the rape out of her therapy sessions with Donna, and she was a woman. Flo didn't know how some of the things she had discussed with Donna would make her feel when she discussed them with a man. She needn't have worried. It was easy and natural to talk to Mirko. She had found that she could talk to him as freely she had with Donna.

At times, she could even talk about issues she had not been willing to share with a woman therapist, such as her relationship with an ex that had continued throughout the last thirty-three years. Flo thought this relationship important because it had somehow escaped the ravages of her control issues. She had never felt the pressures of life, of living in her shoes, when she was with Dario. The outside world disappeared when she was with him. Though they were never meant to be, they understood the reasons behind this and accepted them with grace. They took each moment they were together for the gift that it was. Those times were, as Flo looked back on them in her sessions, the only time she had lived in the moment with no past and no future – just a simple, complete, trusting, caring, and loving now. Surely this must give hope that it could be created in other areas of her life. Mirko agreed. Her therapy had now taken on purpose and direction.

Because of the abandonment by her mother, and the void of not knowing her father, Mirko, maybe by transference, was someone Flo found easy to trust. After the violence she had suffered at the hands of a man, Mirko had a way of creating a safe space for Flo. She was rebuilding trust in men by the safe atmosphere Mirko provided during their sessions. The room was always pleasant. Soft music, mostly nature sounds and harmonies, played softly in the background of each session. The chair or couch was always covered with a soft muted throw blanket. Tissues were always at the ready. No matter how Flo felt when entering Mirko's office, she felt comforted once she settled into the chair.

Mirko never pushed for more than Flo was willing to share in those first months of therapy. Most of her time in therapy had been to create a way for Flo to function again in a world she had withdrawn from for two and a half years. Mirko was taking her therapy in another new direction. She would learn to look to the child she had once been. Flo was reluctant at first. As the time passed, Flo was able to verbalize the fears that were troubling her. After they had been working together for several months, Mirko began Flo's real therapy. Flo had to find her own answers. He was her guide, but he was not her answers. Only Flo held the answers to all the questions in her life.

"Why do you think you have such difficulty with criticism?" Mirko looked at Flo and knew he would have to wait for her to process this question before she would answer. The last several sessions were difficult for Flo. She had begun to see a pattern of behavior that had predated the rape. This pattern was not only self-destructive, but it is what had let her believe in her myth of control. She was ready to see that it was connected, all of it, to the abandonment by her mother. Would she be willing? That was a different story.

"I don't know." Flo was sitting in the chair with her arms and legs crossed. This was a sign to Mirko that she was self-protecting and not ready to let her defenses down. "Yes. You do know. You may not like the answer, but it is there in your mind right now." Mirko sat quiet and still. He knew she would resist, but she had figured it out.

The music in the background was low and melodic. The lights in the office were dimmed. The hum of a privacy machine emitted a soft white noise purr. Flo stared at the clock across the room. It silently told her she had more time left in this session than she wanted. She knew the answer. She had for a while now. She didn't want to speak the words. To say it aloud would negate the coping mechanism she had used all her life. It would mean much of the strife she had gone through was probably of her own making. It would mean she had no defenses left. She sat afraid.

As the minutes passed, Flo finally realized that this was her defining moment. If she didn't do this now, she might not do it at all. She took a deep breath and looked at Mirko. "I don't like criticism because I want everyone to like me. If they don't like me, then they will leave me or make me leave. It also means I have failed somehow. I lost control. I did something wrong. That means I'm no good. I deserved it. I made them leave me." She didn't feel the tears that were streaming down her cheeks; she was numb inside. The effort to say these words made her cold, and she shivered in the comfortably warm room.

"So you deserved to be raped then? You had no control over that. By your reasoning, that was bad, wasn't it?" Mirko leaned slightly forward in his chair, but he did not move too close. He wanted her to think about this question because he would connect it to her past very soon. Flo had started at this question, as he knew she would. Her eyes looked sad and shocked at the same time. She blinked a few times and he knew she was ready.

"No!" No... of course not. I ... it .... No." Flo was confused. Her logic and reasoning did not fit here. Why? She was not in control here. She was not 'bad' here. She began to see. She began to understand.

She began to scream.

After that breakthrough day, Mirko made me work – hard! I had to learn to look inside myself and find the child that was abandoned so long ago. That child was scared, lost, lonely, and afraid that everyone would leave her if she wasn't good enough, or smart enough, or brave enough, or sexy enough, or domestic enough – or ... in control enough. I had to mother this inner child and tell her she was all of those 'enoughs' and more. That it was all right to fail sometimes. She would still be loved. She would still have the 'value' that her mother had not believed she had in that Queens apartment in late summer, 1952.

I am still reassuring that inner child of her worth. It is much easier than before therapy with Mirko. I have been able to see the lack of connection between a mother and child so long ago as a loss. It was never grieved or mourned. It was never resolved or addressed. Even the adults in my life talked about my mother's abandoning me in hushed whispers. It reinforced the negativity of the act. My little mind, my forming psyche, my id, magnified that negativity until it consumed my soul.

I tried to control externally what I could not internally. I pushed emotion out and embraced control. I had only images of a child's version of what is good. I modeled relationships on perceived abandonment.[19] I had actually set myself up for a grand fall. The rape was only a catalyst for what was inevitable...

... my crash in the tunnel.

Florrie at age three. Hampshire, England

Amy Elizabeth Anderson

My Moose.

Fruffles.

Bunny

The magical garden in the grounds of Windsor Castle where I finished the first edit of this book.

The stark reality of a dorm room at Oxford.

Kerry Preston, My Eternal Protector

Len and I in happier times.

My Frankie.

Tommy Farese – my Christmas miracle.

Dear reader,

I am Flo. I am not the 'same' Flo you have been reading about thus far. I am on the way to becoming a true sum of my 'parts' – an integrated being. I have learned that life is not a series of separate events that happen and then disappear. We, each one of us, are a sum of our parts, these events of our lives. I often tell my students that we do not exist alone. Each life event touches us and many others. Sometimes these events change us so subtly that we are unaware of the change. Sometimes these events change us so profoundly that we may no longer be the 'self' we were before. Sometimes we need the help of others to show us the way to navigate life's events. It is all right, and indeed preferable to seek this help. I waited much too long. I am on the upswing of life's pendulum again. I often reflect on how I would be today, who I would be today, if I had asked for help earlier in my life. But I am here now. Whole. Happy. Content. I am still growing, changing, integrating ... like the bud of the rose I once was – I am blooming.

Read on!

Seeing the Light

Chapter One - **Oxford 2001 and 2005**

I don't know what made me apply for a study abroad at Oxford University in England. Maybe I was homesick. I never thought I would be accepted. I mean Oxford – now really. I know I am not the brightest person, and I tend to overreach at times, but I had to do it. I wrote the best damned entrance essay I could, but I knew my chances would be slim. There were thousands applying for 90 spots. There you have it. Flo is dreaming big again.

When the letter arrived from Oxford, my husband had brought it in the house and put it away. He waited until dinner was over and we were relaxing in front of the television with dogs on laps and tea in warmly steaming mugs by our sides. "This came for you today. I think you should plan for a trip soon." He had reached behind him and pulled out a creamy white envelope with a darkly royal blue seal and writing. I stared at it afraid to reach out and touch it - afraid I would be dreaming and wake up... afraid how my life would change if I was not accepted... afraid how my life would change if I was.

With shaking hands I slowly opened the envelope. I didn't want it to rip. It was like the most precious artifact to me. Scanning the page quickly, I saw the word "Congratulations." I had made it. I was going to Oxford!

The adage that says 'be careful what you wish for' is true. Once the excitement of arriving in Oxford had ebbed, and I was medicated correctly so there would be no chance of jet-lag induced mania breaking through, I saw my room. I cried. I literally broke into tears as soon as the grad assistant for the program silently closed the door. I had experienced this same kind of feeling once before. It was on my first day as a student in the university where I now teach, the University at Albany. I had come from a two year college that was local and small. The vastness of Albany had terrified me. I parked my car in what I thought was a safe and easily identifiable place. It was safe, but not quite identifiable because there were four similar spots on the huge campus. I had eventually gone to the campus police in tears and they drove me around the campus until I found my car. Now, several years later, I was crying again. Not because of the vastness, but because of the sparseness and smallness.

My room was three floors up, no elevators, a tiny space with a bed [read mattress on a wood shelf here], a bookshelf, a desk, a small closet, a chair and table, and sink. No toilet. No shower. No tub. There was a window. Had I just joined a nunnery?

I learned this was the typical dorm set up in Oxford. Only upper-classmen and lecturers [professors] had facilities in their rooms. My toilet was up or down one floor. My shower was on my floor. There were no bathtubs. All were shared co-ed facilities. Uggghhhhh!

The dorms were the least of my worries when I learned about the reading lists for my classes. In England one 'reads' for a degree; one does not 'take classes.' The courses I read for were English Literature courses. Two of them, Jane Austen and the Romantic Poets, were chosen by me for specific reasons. I had always loved reading Jane Austen. I had figured, as many students often do, that it would be an easy A. The Romantic Poets was a course I needed to take for my degree. I thought it would be wonderful to take a course with Keats, Shelley, and Byron in England. Sometimes the best laid plans...

I read from morning until night. I ate with a book in my hands. I fell asleep with a book in my hands. I woke up with a book... well, on the floor, but I picked it up and it was in my hands then. The reading lists were extensive. Secondary reading, often lacking in American universities, was *not* lacking in Oxford. The reading was not the only difference in English universities. Classes were different too.

Lectures were in the morning and no matter your course subject, you attended every one. It is the equivalent of our General Education classes. Lateness was not tolerated at all. Older students were at the lecture center doors at every lecture. Students carried an attendance card that was stamped when they entered. There was no chance of sneaking out past these 'guards' either.

If students were late, they were refused entrance and had to stay in the hall until lecture was over to apologize to the professors. No one was ever late more than once. Lectures themselves, could go on forever. Most lasted about three hours.

After lunch you had tutorials with your course professors. The classes were small, with two to six people the norm. You did the reading because each day you were asked questions and had to provide topics for discussion from your views on what you had read.

Professors taught with the Socratic Method. One never knew when it would be his or her turn for this 'interrogation.' It was an intense experience. Most of my students would leave school if I taught this way in America!

Two professors I remember most were Sandie Byrne, Fellow and Tutor of Balliol College, and Simon Kovesi, Senior Lecturer in Romantic Literature and acting Head of English of Oxford Brookes University.

Sandie Byrne is an Austen scholar who authored many books on Austen and other famous British authors. She is the epitome of an upper class British professor: intelligent, classic, and intimidating. I wanted to please her.

Old behaviors poured from my veins. I read every book. I poured through the secondary reading. I tried to book time in the computer room every day. Another difference between American and British universities is the computer rooms. Mine consisted of about a dozen Neanderthal computers that were always booked. Of course, students had to provide their own paper.

Knowing I would not be able to type my final paper in time, I had a plan! I hand wrote it 'Jane Austen' style. It was in the form of a letter. It was written in every space possible, including around the edges when room ran out – true to Austen's letter writing style. This would either make my paper unique enough to get a good grade, or I would fail horribly and skulk away. I got an A.

Simon Kovesi taught me to love poetry. He was a wonderful, but demanding professor. I had to present Keats "Ode on a Grecian Urn" to him and my peers. I read several books with differing interpretations on the Ode, and prepared my presentation.

Our class had about six students. I presented about half way through the class session. I was nervous, but got through it without forgetting anything or stumbling over my words.

When I had finished, Simon looked at me, thought for a minute, and said, "That was a wonderful presentation on this classic and important ode. Yes, it was wonderful – for a first year. Correct me if I am wrong, but you are a graduate student, correct?" He didn't wait for an answer, but proceeded to present on the Ode as it should have been done by me. Yikes!!! A- in that course.

But it was still heaven for me.

I loved it enough to apply and get accepted once more. I began my Masters courses and finished my Doctorate courses at Oxford. I transferred the credits back home easily. I loved every moment of every experience at Oxford. I learned I could focus my mind and achieve my goals. I learned not to fear the unknown. I learned I did not have to control every second to have control. I grew as a person and when I came home after the second semester, I attacked my new goal – teaching.

But first there were the exams ...

Oxford was wonderful and I grew to love that little room.

Eventually, bitten by the Romantic Poet bug, I walked the streets of Oxford in a long flowing coat; collar pulled up, hair streaked blue, and always stopped for a pint at the Bird and Baby. [Eagle and Child pub – home of the Inklings, a literary club in the 1800's]

I visit every year. Last summer I went back and was sad to see my room converted into an office.

I have some wonderful memories from my life there. It inspired me to create a course for a faculty led study abroad - eventually...

Though I still love Jane Austen, it is not as well received in American classrooms as it was in Oxford. I do, however, teach Keats! Every semester in one of my classes, I begin with this Ode. It is a reminder of student days, of England, and of the fact I do not know as much as I think I do!

And I keep in touch with both professors!

Chapter Two - **Doctoral Exams ... and a new diagnosis.**

Courses finished! I could hardly believe it. I was so happy. Then, I read the Doctor of Arts in Humanistic Studies Bulletin. Oh boy! Courses may have been completed, but reading was not. Seventy five books! I had to read seventy five more books! Realistically, I knew I had to do something for the doctoral exams. I knew reading would be part of it. But I was unprepared to find out how much I would need to do to accomplish this overwhelming task of three, three hour written exams and an oral exam a week later.

Though I had begun my transition from student to instructor much earlier, I still had the student mentality of 'how much do I really have to do?' My mind began trying to figure this out. But, I was overwhelmed already, and my mind fell far short of an answer. I determined that I would need to ask a professor. Choosing which one wasn't easy.

I had chosen my exam committee already. I was comfortable with all three of my chosen professors. I knew I would probably get similar answers from each of them. I eliminated one because she was the most difficult to see. I eliminated another because he was most likely unable to give a simple answer.

That left the third, Dr. Leonard Slade. As chair of the Africana Studies department, he was also overseeing the Doctor of Arts in Humanistic Studies program – my program. He was a wonderful man with a beaming smile and a warm demeanor that put students and faculty alike at ease.

I knew I could arrange to see him. I knew, as chair of my exam committee, he would answer any questions I had not on a basis of duty, but because he truly wanted his students to succeed. I made the appointment.

Dr. Slade was not the only resource I had as a doctoral student. I had Marcy Casavant. The Africana Studies secretary held the department together. Thankfully, she was equally as willing to hold grad students together too. She had gotten all of my paperwork in order for the exams and coordinated everything. I only wished she could take them for me! Marcy arranged my meeting, and I waited for the day and time to arrive.

Sitting comfortably in Dr. Slade's cluttered but homey office, I waited until the right time to ask my most important question. I will never forget that moment. I thought, as many of my students think now, that I could get the answer I wanted by the simple act of being candid enough to ask.

Ah well....

Here goes... "Dr. Slade, all those books on that list – well, they are just examples of what I should know a little about for the exams right? How much of them do I really have to read, ummm, know?" My words came out in a tumble, running over each other and coming to rest with a jolt. Then, with eyes as smiling and sparkling as a little boy at Christmas, Dr. Slade looked at me, smiled wide, and said sweetly, "My dear, you have to know all of them." That day I learned never to ask a question if you aren't prepared to hear the answer.

The exams were difficult. I had read every book cover to cover. There were 25 in my major, English; 25 in my minor, Philosophy; and 25 in the Humanities. Some had been used in previous classes, some were by my request, and some were by each professor's request. I struggled. I worried. I was scared too. But with the help of a good, well-rounded education, wonderful instructors, Marcy, and my will to succeed, I passed. I did very well. I lived through both written and oral exams and became stronger because of the experience. I learned what it feels like to succeed.

Now, I need to learn what it feels like to teach...

I did pass the exams. But it was very difficult. As I began my studying I thought the stress was making me manic. I went to see my psychiatrist to see if a medication change was needed.

She talked with me at length and determined she saw no evidence of mania at all. I told her how difficult it was for me to hold a thought or retain what I was reading.

She questioned me some more and asked if I would be willing to try a new medication. She thought she knew what was happening, but taking this medication and reporting the effect it had on me would make the diagnosis correct.

I did take it and slept for two days. I was surprised because it was a stimulant.

When the sleepiness dissipated, I had clarity in thought that was astounding. I could concentrate and read and best of all, I could remember.

The diagnosis?

Adult ADD – Adult Attention Deficit Disorder.

This disorder often coincides with a Bipolar diagnoses, especially in women.[20]

Hmmmm, at least I am normal in something!

Chapter Three - **My First Class**

Standing in the front of the room that first day, I looked out on a sea of empty seats. I had made sure the room would be available and then planned to be there early – very early. Books in place. Markers out. Notes at the ready. What the hell was I doing here? What the hell was I thinking? Teach? Me? Teach? As a student, I was always uncomfortable speaking in front of a class. At least I had the excuse of being a student. A student can be wrong, but now – now was different. I was expected to know what to say. I was lecturing. I was the one who had to teach the course. Me! Oh my God!

Students began arriving and slowly the small lecture room filled with the sounds of muted voices, papers and books opening, and cell phones being checked one last time before class began. I was busying myself with my own papers and books, but watching the faces stretched out before me. It was a sea of humanity. Each student had his or her own cultures, beliefs, loves, lives, plans, dreams, hopes, hurts, wants, and needs. How could I do this? This is too important to get wrong. I'm a Bipolar with ADD and PTSD and panic attacks, borderline traits, and in therapy for God's sake.

How could I even think of teaching?

It was time. The room was silent. Eyes, so many eyes, were looking at me. I walked to the center of the room. I stood calmly for a few seconds. I smiled. I began to speak. A miracle happened. I felt wonderful. Not a manic wonderful, but a true, real, positive, wonderful. I knew at that moment that I was born to do this. I was born to teach. The fear was gone, never to return. I can teach.

The course was Diversity of Voices in Literature and the Arts, CAS 125, and a quarter course. I had gotten last minute notice because I had to fight to get a course to teach at all. Though my major was English, I was not an English Ph. D. student. I was a Doctor of Arts in Humanistic Studies student. The English department was less than hospitable to me. Though the differences in the two degrees are minimal, I had to fight to get into the English courses I needed, and now I had to fight to teach. When I had approached the English department to teach a course, like my peers, I was told that teaching English courses was reserved for English Ph. D, students only. I was the step child who had no place of her own.

Thankfully, when I went to Dr. Slade, who headed the General Education Courses in the College of Arts and Sciences as well as the DA program at the time, he promptly gave me a General Education course to teach. He had faith in me. He believed in me. He still does.

I learned that there is a place for each of us in this world where we are comfortable and at peace. Teaching is that place for me.

> *I will always look back on that moment with wonder and delight. I was so scared. I experienced a true epiphany that day. I found my place in the world. It could have happened sooner, but I am happy that it happened at all. So many of us never find the place we were destined to be. I did. It makes the struggles and trials of life matter less somehow.*

> *I still have problems with the English department. Though I have been teaching for years, have designed new courses for the General Education department – and gotten state approval for them, and designed and implemented a London Study Abroad program which I teach, I am still apparently incapable of teaching an English course.*

Chapter Four - **Teaching since...**

In the many semesters I have taught since that first class, I continue to be amazed that I am actually doing something I truly love. I take that first day of that first class into every new class every new semester. I love that word – new. That word describes teaching to me. New. Every semester is a new chance to experience the feeling and knowledge that I am where I belong.

I have also had the pleasure of a new chair for the end of my doctoral program, now completed, Greg Stevens. He is the assistant dean of the College of Arts and Science, and my department head. Along with Dr. Slade and Professor Jeff Berman, these three peers are the most important people in the story of my true success in academe. I have also had the pleasure of another department secretary, Cindy Endres. Cindy keeps the joy in teaching for me. When I need her help, she is always there.

Teaching has not always been easy. During the first few semesters I taught, I had to fight some of my personal demons that had come to roost in my classroom.

I noticed a very young girl in one class. She sat against a wall in the first row. With each class session she withdrew more and more. It looked like she wanted nothing more than to disappear and become part of the wall she relied on more and more to hold her up. I knew that feeling. I knew that look.

When the realization dawned on me, my heart beat faster and I wanted to run, screaming, from the room. I took deep breaths to calm myself. But, after class, I approached this student and asked her if she needed someone to talk to. I told her she could come to my office about anything and I would find help for her.

That afternoon she came. Words poured out of her like a waterfall. The story she told me was much like my own. She had been raped on campus. She knew the person. A sibling, also a student, was friends with him. She didn't want to report it because of this. She was also struggling with it. Her life was chaotic before being accepted to the university. Dealing with that, and now the rape, was more than her young mind could handle. She was desperate. I felt her pain. It was hard to hear her story and stay calmly in my chair, a solid figure for her to depend on for help. I knew I had to be calm and find help for her. After calls to her advisor and the Counseling Center, she began therapy.

I wish I could say this early intervention helped, but it was too late for her. I watched her decompensate before my eyes. Eventually, the Counseling Center advised that she be committed. Her family kept me posted on her condition for a while. As far as I know, she is still in a mental hospital.

I had not had to deal with being on the other end of rape before.

I was good at being a victim. I had let life victimize me again and again before I realized that my false sense of control was the true victimizer. But this side was different. Her pain had opened up the wounds I had worked so hard to heal. But, it had also done something else. It taught me true empathy.

I incorporated this into my classrooms. I began to see students differently. They were whole beings, not ID numbers in the flesh, or dollar signs personified. I wanted to be open with my students. I wanted them to see me as a person – with flaws – who understands life has many facets.

Teaching is a give and take. It is symbiotic, not parasitic. I too, learn and grow because I freely open myself to my students. I let them know me as a person. I let them know I see them as more than their university ID's. My students know I am Bipolar. I tell them. They know I lost a child. They know about my rape. If they have questions about these things, I answer them as best I can. It opens a dialogue that is genuine and honest. The students lose fear in the entity 'professor.' They open their minds and truly learn.

I learn from them too. In his book, <u>Dying to Teach</u>, Jeff Berman says, "Education is reciprocal: teachers learn from their students just as students learn from their teachers." [Berman 3] I was lucky enough to have Professor Berman as my teacher. I took every course he taught.

I would be dishonest if I said that my teaching style was uniquely mine. I have had many professors in my tenure as a student. I have lived through professors who thought students were so far beneath them that they could not differentiate the students from the dog shit they stepped in that day.

I have had professors who had passed their expiration date. You would recognize them easily enough. They are the ones you see shuffling down hallways as ghosts of themselves past, wondering if this tenure they have had behind ivied walls will ever end. Their enthusiasm gone long ago, they can no longer remember when, or if, they had it.

I have had professors who exist only to see how much hell they can reign down upon students. They treat teaching as one of Dante's rings of hell especially created for them. Students become penitents.

I have had professors who thought they were spawned from Mt. Olympus, a descendent of Zeus himself. Students were required to be in awe of them during every class ... and if they passed in the hallways.

I have had professors who hated the social interaction of teaching. Many types fall into this category, from those who thought only research would be required of them to those who had to choose a career and chose poorly. They see students as an annoyance. Their office hours are nonexistent – emails go unanswered – and they smile only on the final day of class.

Happily, I have also had professors who were caring and nurturing. Some were awe inspiring. These are the classes students wanted to attend. Every assignment was completed, not because it had to be, but because it was a way to prolong the feeling of inspiration imparted in the classroom. Students in these classrooms wanted to do the work required, and do it well.

These professors left 'bits' of themselves in the students' psyches. Often, students would remember, at some later date, some bit of wisdom from these professors and it made them richer intellectually. These are the professors whose courses filled quickly once registration opened. Wait lists were long, permission numbers were few. Those that 'got in' considered themselves fortunate. They were.

I learned to teach from all of these professors, both the good and the bad. Over time I became more and more refined in the theory and practice, the pedagogy, of teaching. From my own experiences as a student, and as a human being who was sometimes struggling in the lessons of life, I learned empathy in the classroom. In the last chapter, I said I was born to teach. This is true. It is the one thing I have done in my life that 'felt' right. It did not require thought or effort, but rather flowed through me as if in my blood. When I am in the classroom, the world outside does not exist. I am in the moment. It is an ineffable feeling.

The most effective teachers I have had were also empathic teachers. In Jeff Berman's book, <u>Empathic Teaching</u>, he states five ways teachers make a difference in students' lives.

"Teachers instill confidence in their students ... teachers help students to personalize knowledge ... teachers who make a difference in their students' lives are friendly and accessible ... teachers who make a difference are willing to acknowledge what they have learned from their own life experiences, including, when appropriate, events that are rarely spoken about in the classroom ... teachers who make a difference in their students' lives remain part of their lives, even when students no longer see them. Students internalize these teachers." [Berman 13-14]

I know I make a difference. I also know that teaching has made a difference in me. I learned that if you hold the best part of people you admire close to your heart, you can never be abandoned.

Until I read <u>Empathic Teaching</u>, I had no idea how much Professor Berman influenced me. I follow the five ways teachers can make a difference in my teaching. I did so before reading the book. I do so instinctively. My life experiences, along with the nurturing environment I found in Professor Berman's classroom, not only inspired me to teach, but taught me how. This is a debt I intend to repay by continuing to reach out to every student in my classes and make them feel safe, understood, listened to, and willing to learn.

Chapter Five - **London calling.**

When I became comfortable with my teaching, I realized that I had more to give. I wanted to take my teaching on the road so to speak. I spoke to the Study Abroad department in the university and set out to design a new course. That I could teach in England was a plus for sure, but I wanted to give students the ability to take a General Education course outside the university walls. I wanted to open the study abroad to freshmen and EOP students who normally would not participate in studying in another country.

I created an Understanding the Arts course. I called it 'Origins of the British Imagination.' I poured my heart, and my love of England, into its creation. However, my timing was not the best. The pound was up against the dollar so there was no way to make the course affordable to students. I did find a way to teach the course at the university until I could take it across the pond. I, with the help of Dr. Leonard Slade and Marcy Casavant in the Africana Studies department, had it approved for a General Education course at the University. It gave me a chance to perfect the course and tailor it for a study abroad.

In 2009, I took my first group to London. I had fulfilled another dream. I was teaching in London. I had made it happen. Well, not alone. I had the wonderful help of Danielle Leonard and the Study Abroad office. They believed in me. They guided me. They advised me. When needed, they even cried with me when the best laid plans fell through that first summer of 2008.

This was another fear I had faced and overcome. I would never have tried such an ambitious endeavor earlier in my life. It opened me to failure. It did fail, before I ever left the country, but I didn't run from the failure. I can't control the pound! I didn't give up. I didn't break down. I had several bumps along the road before that first London Study Abroad happened. Some frustrated me. Some hurt me deeply because I learned that interaction with some faculty is reminiscent of the cliques of junior high school. But I never let go of my dream that I could do this, and do it well.

I learned that the world can truly be your oyster if you let fear of failure fly coach!

The first study abroad was wonderful. Students in the program made friends with peers in London that they have maintained to this day. They have also bonded with each other.

A dear friend of mine in London, Bea Tollman, owns a chain of beautiful boutique hotels. She arranged elegant afternoon teas in three of her hotels for my group. Her hotels are filled with exquisite hand-picked artwork. It was a wonderful act of kindness and generosity on her part. The students in this first group still miss those teas. The new students look forward to them. The simple act of 'taking tea' has a calming effect on the souls of any ages. The wonderful comfort of the Red Carnation hotels, and the care of the staff, makes my students feel welcome in a place so far away from home. Bea and her staff have helped to make my course the success it is.

Chapter Six **Family and Friends**

Throughout my life I have been blessed with wonderful family and friends who have helped me through the difficult times and celebrated with me during the good times. They may not have always understood me, but they were there. It is impossible to mention everyone here so I am taking the liberty of choosing a few examples, and thanking all for being in my life.

My grandmother, Lillian; aunt, Margaret; and great-grandmother, Emily, gave me what I needed to make it through the worst times in my life: a belief in myself, which though shaken many times, was just buried, and surfaced during therapy; a love of England that made me instinctively seek it out when I was at my lowest points; and a sense of comportment that has served me well.

My sister, Debbie, has seen me at my worst and still speaks to me. Her sense of forgiveness, or of family duty, is more than I deserve.

My cousin George, who is the most wonderful dancer in the world, has danced me through troubled times again and again though he has troubles of his own.

My uncle George and Aunt Charlotte have shown me that sometimes true love prevails, just like in fairytales.

My mother in law, Margie is the woman of strength I aspire to be.

My husband Brian grounds me. In the most manic of times he tethers me to reality.

My son, Lenny, has been there for me when we 'traded places' and I was the child. He parented me better than I have parented him at times. [That story is for another book.]

My son, Bryan, has taught me that parental bonds don't need blood.

To my nephew Chris, you have taught me to look at the inside, not just what is visible.

Jen, first my student, then my friend; our bond came from the sense of similarity in life experiences. You have shown me that wisdom knows no age.

Jordan, you have touched my heart. From the moment you took that first class with me I felt I knew you. In London, I did get to know you. I realized then that you reminded me of my little girl, my Amy. Had she lived, I am sure she would have been very much like you. Thank you for letting me see what might have been. [Burberry forever!]

Lauren, I thank you for being my 'reader.' You have encouraged me more than you know. At times when I had no words left, your enthusiasm let me know I did. [Yorkie's rule!]

Annie, you have been my friend for a long time. You have quietly imparted your wisdom and waited until I understood. You have let me come to realizations on my own. You have always had faith. You held mine in your heart until I was ready to take it back. Thank you.

Tiann, my best friend, you are a true example of giving. You have so much love and you give it so freely, expecting nothing back. Your heart is filled with empathy and compassion. If I could 'pick' a mother, I would pick you!

Bea, you have made me feel at home every time I visit London. You have created a world where everyone is special.

Malcolm [and Lindsay] you and your staff have made me feel well when I was ill, welcomed my guests graciously, and made me feel like I had a second home. I am blessed to know all of you.

Nathan, you are my next husband – don't forget that!

Peter, you are my rock when in London.

To the Umi staff – my London Study Abroad is a success because of each and every one of you who go out of your way to help and do more than what is required. Thank you Steve, Gavin, and Yogi.

To Jamie, you have made sure I get to where I am supposed to be when I am in London. I look forward to our talks. London, at night, is better seen in a Black Taxi! Next pint is on me.

To Kerry Preston, guardsman 1st Battalion Coldstream Guards, and my Eternal Protector: You keep me safe in London, and even if miles apart, I know you are there... I know with a phone call you will protect me from harm. I feel safe in the knowledge you are a part of my world.

To Alex Tollman, you are an amazing and wonderful young woman. You are much like your grandmother in more ways than you know. I hope our friendship keeps growing. Bbar awaits!

To Dereck Albuquerque, keep the Galpin Peak in stock...and your charm and manner at Bbar!

To Kristin, and Jane, her mum, I love you both. I think of you daily. Readers, go to this website and support CoppaFeel... a breast cancer charity for young women. They help save lives. www.coppafeel.org [A portion of the proceeds of the sale of this book will be given to CoppaFeel.]

To the Monster Maxx, you are a truly wonderful person. I am so glad you came into my life.

Finally, there is Tommy Farese. You have given me one of the greatest gifts of all – a chance to go back to the missed holidays of childhood and imprint them with joy and happiness. Though you are no longer with Trans Siberian Orchestra, you have formed a wonderful new group ... The Kings of Christmas. I know it will be successful. Readers, their first CD should be available now.

Their website is www.thekingsofchristmas.com

I wrote a fairy tale for you as my thank you. You have kindly given permission for me to reprint it here.

So, thank you again, for ...

THE GIFT

There once was a boy who wanted to be a man, but he was confused. How do you become a man? He didn't think it had to do with age. There were certainly many men, all of different ages, around him. He knew it must be more than that.

Maybe it had to do with hard work. He thought about his father. The boy knew his father was a man. His father worked very hard. He knew his father was a good man, but with all the hours he had to work, he had little time for the boy who wanted to be a man. His uncles, and some of his friends' fathers, hardly worked at all. They had time for showing a boy how to be a man, but their time was spent in other ways - sometimes dangerous ways. But, thought the boy, they had money and very nice things like new cars and nice watches and clothes that didn't come from the thrift shop or hand me downs.

Maybe it had to do with money, with things. He thought about that too. He wanted nice things. He wanted to be noticed. He didn't like being laughed at or made fun of by the older boys who, to him, were very nearly men. Money could do a lot. Maybe money did make you a man, he thought.

The boy grew. As he grew he tried to find the measure of a man in many ways. Some he was proud of, and some he was not. At times he felt he was a man, and at times he knew he was not. He made many friends and some enemies. He found new love and lost old love. Years went by and he was comfortable in his heart. He rarely thought about the boy in him who once wished to become a man. Getting older sometimes makes us forget about the child that still exists inside every one of us. His life went on.

At the same time the boy was growing and trying to find out how to be a man, a girl was growing too. Abandoned by her mother, she grew in fear. Who would love her? How could someone love a girl whose own mommy didn't love? This little girl grew up wondering how to make people love her enough to stay.

Was it to be good? She tried to be as good as she could be, but, after all, she was a little girl, and little girls were not good all the time. Every time she was scolded she believed she would never be good enough to love.

Was it to make people happy? She tried to do everything that was possible for a little girl to do to make everyone around her happy. Alas, she found that what made one person happy would not please another person. She felt defeated, but would not give up.

She, like the little boy, grew up. She tried in many ways to find out what it was to be loved. She found love for a time here and there. Sometimes she didn't love herself, but she never counted herself when she was looking for her version of love. She, like the boy, forgot about the inner child. Life went on.

Both the little boy and the little girl lived in their worlds created by the child inside each of them. Until, one day, when both of them didn't realize it, the children inside of them decided they would meet.

The girl, now a woman, sat alone in the dark. It was Christmas Eve. Life had taught the woman to fear holidays. This holiday was exceptionally painful. Her own little girl, whom she loved very much, was born right before this holiday. But, she had died years ago. This left the woman bitter and sad. The only light in her life was the glow of the TV in her living room.

Suddenly, music filled the room! Lights sparkled in floating rhythm and danced about her. The woman looked at the TV screen and saw the little boy who wanted to be a man. He, too, was grown.

The little boy and the little girl had now met. The boy's voice called to the girl and she listened. She heard the words he sung to her. And, like most magical moments, this one ended as quickly as it had begun. But the magic itself went on.

The woman began to let the light of the holiday inside her again. She went out into the world once more and began to look for the love she sought, but not from the outside, from the inside. Love, after all, begins inside us.

Then, one day, the little girl decided to return the gift to the little boy. Appropriately, it was another Christmas holiday season. The TV glowed with the magical light once more. The little boy, grown, was singing the same song.

The little girl inside the woman said now was the time to say thank you for the gift of love he had given to her all those years ago. And, as we do now, the woman searched for a way to find him on the internet. When she did, she merely stated in a few lines what that Christmas Eve long ago had given her because of his song.

The little boy, now grown, read the note and smiled. A feeling of magic, much like the magic that had happened to the woman when she had heard his voice those many years ago, began to wash over the now grown boy. He knew, really knew, what it was to be a man.

The End

I learned that love exists.

There is no way I can put on paper all the wonderful people who have helped me get through my life to this point. If I did not mention you, it is not because I don't remember. I do. I am grateful. I thank you.

Chapter Seven - **Looking Ahead**

So, here I am now... still evolving. I have an understanding of life that many do not. I have seen and experienced many things. I am different, but I am also the same. Sometimes I think I am the person I should have become years ago if I had not been born into the 'circumstances' of life on that day in June. No matter, I have become that person now and I am grateful.

I have entitled this chapter 'Looking Ahead," and by those words, I have misled my readers... I am looking back. I know now that you cannot look ahead without first looking at what has been. The past defines us; whether good or bad, our future is connected – no, directed by our past. We either integrate life's experiences into who we are or we externalize them and they affect us over and over again until we break – until we crash.

I do not know what my future holds. I know that no matter what happens, I have a stronger base on which to handle life. I am becoming earthquake-proof. I know what I would like my future to look like. I have created goals to help make my dreams realities. I am, however, no longer under the assumption that I have total control, or that I can make things happen. Life is unpredictable. Life happens. We deal with what comes.

I look forward to many years of being able to do what I love most – teach. As I said in Chapter 4, it is my calling. It is my passion. I make a difference. I touch humanity and it touches me – a lesson learned from Princess Diana. Of learning, I know I learn much more from my students than they learn from me. This is how it should be. Life is a learning experience for all of us, and we all get to grade ourselves eventually. My grandmother once told me that when you stop learning, you might as well be dead. She was right. She was usually right.

It is in the act of learning about life that we fulfill our purpose. Our grade comes, hopefully in old age, when we are waiting for our own 'last goodbye.' It is at that point when we will perform our own final self-assessment and grade our own lives. My students often ask me if I have any regrets. I don't hesitate when I say no. I have not always made the best choices. I have not always done the right thing. However, each choice or action I made I own. All of them helped to make me who I am now. How can I regret them? It is not what we have done that we regret, but rather what we wish we had done. When we grade ourselves at the end of our lives, we will deduct points for that.

You may want to reread this...

There is a quiz at the end of your life.

I learned to understand the frightened woman in that small cell who had a rosebud that finally bloomed.

I love you mom!

She was sitting in the grass in the Queen's Garden at Windsor Castle. The day was sunny with a gentle breeze carrying the smell of wildflowers through the summer air. Her skirt, a deep rich purple, was spread around her. She thought she looked like she was floating on a lily pad through the sea of perfectly manicured green grass. It was beautiful and peaceful here. She thought of her life and how she had come to this point. She had traveled a long road, but she had managed the journey and now, sitting here with peace in her heart, she put pen to paper to finish the final chapters of her book... her story... her life. She heard the plane overhead and looked up. She thought she saw a face in one of the windows. It was a small boy. As she looked, he pressed his lips on the glass and she imagined the touch of the soft kiss he had sent her. She felt like a princess.

EPILOGUE

By no means is this book a comprehensive view of my life. There were normal, happy times and periods of calm to go along with what you have read here in these pages. We are made up of moments in time. None are exclusionary; all are important. I have chosen to share some of these moments here... that is all.

We shape our lives by how we define these moments. Sometimes, we crash. It may take a while for us to recover. What I hope my readers can see in the words of my story is, though we may have our own unique crashes, we can recover. Healing is not linear. We may slide backwards before moving ahead. This is all right. This does not mean we are any less worthy of the new life we are trying to build. I try to use this idea of life's moments in my teaching.

This phenomenon of crashing happens more often than I thought. Students' crash and burn, for many unique reasons; most young adults do not have the coping skills needed to come out of their tunnels and back into the light. The students become literally withdrawn from not only classes, but life. Through my teaching, I let them know there is always a way out if you look for it. I encourage them to seek help. I was in the dark for much longer than I should have been. I wish someone had told me there was help. I would have grabbed it with both hands and embraced it with my very soul.

We are amazing and complex creatures. We have the ability to heal ourselves. Many times, when we do not believe we can go on, our minds process what we do not believe we can handle. Sometimes you need a guide. I have learned this through my experiences, therapy, and most of all - teaching.

I hope that my readers see themselves in my words. Knowing there are others out there, who hurt at times too, sometimes comforts us. It is a mental affirmation that we are all in this thing called life, together. We all have pain. We all want comfort. In that, we are as similar as we are different.

Go out and seek the light you have been missing in your life.

Postscript

Some of the portion of this book, in the chapters after The Crash, came from a diary I kept in the months after the rape. I wrote in rants and raves, in prose and poems, and wrote in questions ... mostly, why? I had not, until the writing of this book, looked inside that diary. I kept it high on a shelf in a closet. I knew, one day, I would read it again. I began by writing around that certain chapter until I felt strong enough to do what I needed.

I accessed the diary in small steps. First, I just acknowledged the diary was there; this had not been done in a long time. Then, I thought about the day I would reach for it on that shelf. Finally, I took it down. It sat, unopened, for longer than I would like to admit. It was next to my chair in the living room. I could acknowledge it now, but I would turn from it quickly. I did not want to touch it – or let it touch me. Then, one day, I opened its pages and the 'hold' it seemed to have on me for such a long time, disappeared ...

I was free!

Author's Notes:

Note One

There is one person I have omitted from this story. I have done so because he was dying and I wanted to give him privacy in his last days.

He was a part of my life for over thirty years.

He was my soul.

He was my haven and comfort.

He was the first 'adult' relationship I formed.

He was truly proud of me even when I was not proud of myself.

He asked nothing from me, yet would give me anything.

Dario was dying as I wrote this book. He is gone now. Cancer. The word hurt. His family hurt. His friends hurt. I hurt. I could not imagine a world in which he is not breathing the same air as I do. He has filled every empty space in my heart and will always do so. The bravery and dignity he showed since his diagnosis, through his treatments, and unto his death, was remarkable. I can only aspire to be half of what he has been. Someday, I will tell his story.

... someday... quite soon.

Note Two

I felt it important to let my readers see the words from the Christmas song that gave me back holidays. It is from, and by, Trans-Siberian Orchestra.

If these words touch you, like they did me, Google the band.

"THIS CHRISTMAS DAY"

So, tell me Christmas
Are we wise
To believe in things we never
see

Are prayers just wishes in
disguise
And are these wishes being
granted me

For now I see
The answering
To every prayer I've prayed

She's coming home this
Christmas Day

So tell me Christmas
Are we kind
More this day than any other
day

Or is it only in our mind
And must it leave when you
have gone away

It's different now
It's changed somehow
And now you're here to stay

She's coming home this
Christmas Day

All at once the world
It doesn't seem the same
And in a single night
You know it all has changed
And everything is now as it
should be

I have the ornament
I have the perfect tree
I have a string of lights
I have a chance to see
Everything that my heart
thought could be

For of all the dreams
You were the first I knew
And every other one
Was a charade of you
You stayed close when I was
far away

In the darkest night
You always were the star
You always took us in
No matter who we are
And so she's coming home
this Christmas Day

Sung by Tommy Farese
Written by Paul O'Neill, et al Trans-Siberian Orchestra

NOTES:

1 Grasslands Hospital: It is now Westchester County Medical Center. It was originally an Army hospital that was given to the state and renamed Grasslands Hospital. It continued under that name until 1977. It rebranded as Westchester Country Medical Center in 1978. [Wikipedia]

2 Bedford Hills Correctional Institution for Women - Bedford Hills correctional Institution is a women's prison in Bedford hills, Westchester County, New York. [Though, at the time my mother was an inmate, it was called Westfield State Farm, I have always heard it called Bedford Hills – a name change occurred in 1970.] It is a maximum security facility for females 16 years old or over. (New York State Archives)

3 Abandonment: According to the authors of Beyond Empathy, early relationships are what make us human. It is where we learn that "*I* and *me* are separate and distinct from *you.*" [Erskine 5] We learn our internal needs will be taken care of through external contacts who recognizing those needs. When this relationship is interrupted at an early stage in a child's development, the child must self-parent. The child believes that no one will be there for him or her. This leads the child to detach from emotions and/or emotional attachments because there is now an expectation that no one will be there. This is "avoidant attachment."[6]

Because we, as human beings, develop our sense of empathy and compassion through emotional attachment to other human beings, a child abandoned by a parent, especially a mother who normally is the first line in this development, never develops a sense of self.

As an adult, this 'child being,' when traumatized, has no coping mechanism in place. This 'child being's' psyche splinters even further. This adult may wonder, as I did, why he or she cannot just get on with the process of living. After the rape, I wondered why I just couldn't go on like I had done so many times before. I had 'lived' through my daughter's death. I had seen my son's face as the police told him the details of his father's death. I had lost my mother, my father, my great-grandmother, grandmother, grandfather, uncles, aunts, pets, and survived. I could not go on now. I thought I must be 'bad' somehow. That I had done something so awful that I deserved what had happened to me. I tried to push what had happened even further away from reality by imagining it was a dream, or that it had not really happened to me, or that it wasn't so bad. In effect, I had no way to process this kind of trauma. I could no longer parent the child inside me. I broke from reality. I crashed.

4 Being 'good' to be in control: See note 20.

5 Control after abandonment: See note 20.

6 Battered Women Syndrome: According to Dr. Leonore Walker's, the developer of the concept of battered women's syndrome, there are four general characteristics of the syndrome: The woman believes that the violence was or is her fault. The woman has an inability to place responsibility for the violence elsewhere. The woman fears for her life and/or her children's lives. The woman has an irrational belief that the abuser is omnipresent and omniscient. [http://www.rainn.org]

7 Reyes Syndrome: Please check out the National Reyes syndrome web pages at: [http://www.reyessyndrome.org]

8 "Geisinger Medical Center: Since 1915, Geisinger Medical Center has been known as the region's resource for high quality healthcare, providing care to more than two million residents throughout central and northeastern Pennsylvania. We have recruited top physicians from across the country to join our experts in virtually every medical field, all working to provide you with the most experienced, most compassionate care.

Geisinger also offers some of the most advanced technology in the country, a Level I Trauma Center; a 5-helicopter LifeFlight® program and clinical research facilities. Physicians throughout Pennsylvania, as well as New York and New Jersey, refer their most complex cases to the 404-bed Geisinger Medical Center, a tertiary and quarternary medical center recently named one of the Top 100 Hospitals in the country.

The medical center has also been designated as a Magnet hospital by the American Nurses Credentialing Center (ANCC). These credentials represent just a few of the national awards and distinctions that Geisinger has earned to become one of the most respectable hospitals in the country. When you need us, we'll be here." [GMC web site]

9 Flu shots 1979: A book was published in 1978. It was titled: The Swine Flu Affair, Decision Making on a Slippery Disease. Panic ensued with a mass refusal to be inoculated for the 1978-1979 flu season – the season that my daughter died. Later that year, just in time for the 1979-1980 flu season, the 60 Minutes report on the 1976 swine flu vaccines, was aired.

You can read this book online at: Http://www.nap.edu/openbook.php?record_id=12660&page=1

10 Suicide: In his book, <u>Surviving Literary Suicide</u>, Jeff Berman posts the ten common characteristics of suicide as posited by the late professor Edwin Shneidman.[Berman 54-55] I am posting them here for my readers who may see themselves in these words. I did. Every single one of these characteristics was exhibited by me in the two and a half years that I was actively suicidal. It is a profound and enlightening experience to read these astounding words and know that I was not alone, as I believed I was, but others had experienced these feelings enough times to be studied and understood.

1. The common stimulus in suicide is unendurable psychological pain.
2. The common stressor in suicide is frustrated psychological needs.
3. The common purpose of suicide is to seek a solution.
4. The common goal of suicide is cessation of consciousness.
5. The common emotion in suicide is hopelessness/helplessness.
6. The common internal attitude toward suicide is ambivalence.
7. The common cognitive state in suicide is constriction.
8. The common action in suicide is egression.
9. The common interpersonal act in suicide is communication of intention.
10. The common consistency in suicide is with lifelong coping patterns.

11 PTSD and Flashbacks: PTSD occurs when a traumatic event threatens your physical and/or mental integrity. According to the DSM, the severity and duration of PTSD is especially severe if the trauma is "of human design."[DSM 464] Rape is of human design. I agree with the DSM's assessment.

Flashbacks, or random reliving of the traumatic event, are especially disturbing and vivid if the trauma was caused by another person. Because of this, there are other disorders and features associated with PTSD. For example, insomnia, hypervigilance, exaggerated startle reflexes, and difficulty concentrating can change a trauma victim's personality and alter his or her way of life significantly. Other disorders that can follow or occur at the same time as PTSD are: Major Depressive Disorder, Substance Related Disorders, Panic Disorder, Agoraphobia, Obsessive-Compulsive Disorder, Generalized Anxiety Disorder, Social Phobia, Specific Phobia, and Bipolar Disorder.[DSM 465]

12 Trauma and writing: In her article, *From Trauma to Writing*, Professor Marion MacCurdy, of Ithaca College, states that writing about trauma not only produces better writing, but it also allows the writer to connect the emotions and images of the traumatic event. This produces a therapeutic healing in the writer. I know it does help me. I also know professors who use this type of writing in the classroom with amazing results in good writing and the added benefit of students who feel they have learned not only coursework, but something about themselves and their peers. Though I do not teach this type of writing per se, I do get writing of this type from my students. I have gotten positive feedback from them upon completion of their writing.

13 Trial: I am constrained in speaking about the events of my rape and the subsequent civil trial. Part of the settlement was the signing of a confidentiality agreement.

14 Death and closure: I do not believe in closure. The closure I received in holding my beloved Yorkie, Fruffles, was purely one of physicality. I 'held' my daughter through my dog. I had always regretted not being able to hold Amy one more time. I don't have that regret any longer. For that, I am grateful. I do not have closure in the death of my child. Closure means a sense of finality, an end. It has not ended for me. There is no sense of finality. I think of her very day. I will always feel her with me.

15 Cancer Sniffing Dogs: There is a web page that has the results of the study done on this ability of dogs to sniff out cancers. There is also a podcast and other links. See bibliography.

16 ADH: The following web page has wonderful information on ADH and DCIS. The two may overlap, but you cannot be treated [other than the usual recommendation for preventative double mastectomies] until DCIS [stage 0 breast cancer] is found. The problem is that they mimic each other and it is the call of the pathologist to make the diagnosis. The small amount of breast tissue taken in biopsies allow for a large margin of error. http://www.breastcancer.org/symptoms/types/dcis/diag nosis.jsp 166

17 Bipolar Disorder 1: According to the DSM, bipolar disorder 1 is "characterized by one or more Manic or Mixed episodes, usually accompanied by Major Depressive Episodes." [DSM 4, 345] I am bipolar 1. I am also a rapid cycling bipolar. This means I cycle many times a year, and often several times a day as well. It also means that seasonal changes affect me. I am sensitive to the time changes of travel too. Jet lag does not tire me, but can trigger mania or mixed episodes. According to the DSM, "women comprise 70% to 90% of individuals with a rapid cycling pattern." [DSM 4, 427] I am, therefore, a 'normal' bipolar 1.

18 Bipolar children: In the book, The Bipolar Child, by Demitri and Janice Papolos, some of the signs of bipolar disorder in children mimic ADHD or ADD. There is often impulsive behaviors and control issues that can be misdiagnosed or attributed to the child being called difficult or high-strung. I was both. I do have adult ADD which usually goes hand in hand with Bipolar 1. Because we have 20-20 vision in hindsight, I do believe I was bipolar as a child.

19 Borderline Personality Disorder: According to my doctors and therapists I have Borderline traits, not full blown Borderline Personality Disorder. I knew I had these traits before I was diagnosed. In the months after Princess Diana died, many rushed to publish books about every personal aspect of her life. I read them all. One in particular intrigued me. The author stated he thought the princess had Borderline Personality Disorder.He listed clinical symptoms and her symptoms. I thought he was writing about me. This could be because Princess Diana had been abandoned by her mother too.

This is, apparently, almost a prerequisite for this disorder. In the DSM, it is defined as "a pervasive pattern of instability of interpersonal relationships, self-image, and affects, and marked impulsivity that begins before adulthood and is present in a variety of contexts."[DSM 706]

People with this disorder react, in uncontrolled ways, to any perceived abandonment. Even if the abandonment occurs in the natural order of things, such as my therapist, Donna, moving to another state for a better job, the reaction will be over inflated. Notice how Donna waited until the last possible moment to inform me. All her other clients had known. If I would have been informed, she knew there would have been a good chance of my leaving therapy to 'get back at her for leaving me.'

There is a tendency for those with this disorder to self-harm. Princess Diana used cutting. I used it too. I also pull out toe nails. Ah, I can see my readers squirming at that one. Isn't that a form of torture outlawed by the Geneva Convention? Well, yes. But in the mind of a Borderline personality, it is both a release and an affirmation.

My mind would get so caught up in preventing abandonment, keeping control, being "good," that I longed for a moment, a second, where there was nothing in my mind but emptiness. At the same time, I didn't feel like I was attached to the world, to the living. The act of pulling out that toenail, though causing a brief intense pain, both affirmed I was alive and cleared my mind. I'm sure it did the same for Princess Diana and any other person who self-harms to feel.

20 Adult ADD: Adult ADD is usually not associated with hyperactivity. It is the attention deficit, usually noticed by others first, that brings adults to seek help. According to the DSM, adults with ADD have difficulty completing tasks. They may move from task to task leaving none completed. This happens in the workplace and in the home. They may also be easily distracted by stimuli that most people would not register. In social settings, they may not listen to others or that may shift conversation frequently.[DSM 84-85] For me, it was not being able to hold a job for too long. I would leave as soon as I got bored. When friends and family began asking me for reasons why I couldn't seem to stay in one job, I usually deflected them. When I was diagnosed, I was already well into my therapy, which was actually masking some of my behavioral symptoms. I look back on my flight from place to place and job to job in a way that is bittersweet. I missed so many opportunities, but I have gained more experiences and experience than most.

BIBLIOGRAPHY

American Psychiatric Association. Diagnostic and Ststistical Manual of Mental Disorders. Arlington: american Psychiatric Association, 2007.

Anderson, Charles M and Marion M MacCurdy. Writing and Healing. Urbana: National Council of Teachers of English, 2000.

Berman, Jeffrey. Dying to Teach. New York: State University of New York Press, 2007.

Berman, Jeffrey. Empathic Teaching. Amherst: University of Massechuesetts Press, 2004.

Berman, Jeffrey. Surviving Literary Suicide. Amherst: University of Massachucetts Press, 1999.

Casabrian, Brian, www.casabrian.com

Erskine, Richard G, Janet P Moursund and Rebecca L Trautmann. Beyond Empathy. New York: Routledge, 1999.

Geisinger-Medical-Center,
http://www.geisinger.org/locations/gmc/

"Karen Ann Quinlan Memorial Foundation," History Page. December-12, 2008. http://www.karenannquinlanhospice.org/history.htm

"National Reyes Syndrome Foundation," Information Page. December 21. 2008. http://www.reyessyndrome.org.what.html.

New York State Archives, http://www.archives.nysed.gov Papolos, Demitri and Janice. <u>The Bipolar Child</u>. New York: Broadway Books, 2002

Science-Netlinks, http://www.sciencenetlinks.com/sci_update.php?DocID=2 91